Get to Know Me ...

NAME: Diana Tenured
I LIKE TO BE CALLED: Diana — Queen of the world
OCCUPATION: Executive Assistant

IMPORTANT PEOPLE (FAMILY AND FRIENDS):
Jerry, Mom, Debbie, Yvonne, Penny, Lynn, Gary, Sue, Heavily, Tammy, Scott, Carla, Andrea, everyone who's touched our lives...

FAVORITES

MOVIE: Ghost Whisperer
TV SHOW: Minnesota Cotain App; Mentalist; The Bold wife;
BOOK: Devotionals; Crosswords
MUSIC: Country & Blues
SPORT: Patriots & Red Sox
COLOR Aquamarine
FOODS: Filet Mignon; Atti; Coffee
ACTIVITIES/HOBBIES: Garden; refinishing

QUOTE OR SAYING:
"Trust & Rely on God" & "In Gods Time"

PETS TOO!: Serena & Wyan

AT HOME I USE:

- ☐ GLASSES
- ☐ CT LENSES
- ☐ HEARING AID
- ☐ DENTURES
- OTHER: _____

I UNDERSTAND INFORMATION BEST WHEN:
Told how to do something constructively — not critically

ACHIEVEMENTS OF WHICH I AM PROUD:
Sobriety; working the steps, taking her own meds seriously, being a better friend

THINGS THAT STRESS ME OUT:
Jerry; not finishing stuff on my todo list; bad drivers

THINGS THAT CHEER ME UP:
Cold Stone Creamery, Friends, my Kitties, Franklyn Snickers, Sunny days, lunch

OTHER THINGS I'D LIKE YOU TO KNOW ABOUT ME:
Very strong faith, bubbly, strong willed, determined, very organized, thrifty person, Loves to laugh & — even at Tomatoes, Great friend, always intent of sister. Devoted partner.

Diana's *"Get to Know Me"* wall chart from her many months at Mass General.

God Never Moved

A Couple's Journey Through Fire to Life

Diana Tenney and Jerry Laperriere

(With Laura Graves and Randall Surles)

Copyright © 2023 Diana Tenney & Jerry Laperriere
All rights reserved.
ISBN: 9798857024539

Interior design by Ink Blots, Amagansett, NY
Cover design by Fly-By-Night Artworks, Brooklyn, NY

Feel free to contact Diana through Facebook below, or:
dianatenney@comcast.net

Visit Diana's Burn Survivor Facebook page for a variety of links to videos about surviving burn injuries. ***God Never Moved – A Couples Journey Through Fire to Life***:
https://www.facebook.com/profile.php?id=100095591526205

To our families, friends, burn survivors, and medical professionals who have been beside us on this rollercoaster journey.

God Never Moved

The First Spark

The heart of the flame is a place of stillness, nothing can touch it, and yet it touches everything. It destroys everything and creates everything, everything is absorbed within it. Breathe in and out now. There is a never-ending warmth inside the flame a cocoon of softness, all enveloping.
What is left when everything has burned down?
—Luigi Gatti Bonati

<u>Diana</u>

When I was fifty-four years old, I was burned on over ninety percent of my body.

I almost died.

But I didn't.

Jerry and I went through hell and back, but we survived. That's not surprising to me. We were strong people before the fire, and that was evident in everything that passed after.

We met the night before 9/11. Sounds like the start of a love story, doesn't it? And, in a way, it is.

In 2001, I was living on Long Island and was out of a job since the industry food service company (manufacturing china and flatware) that I had been working for as a sales rep had been bought out.

By September, my unemployment was running out and my job prospects were still dim. I knew about a large industry food service trade show set in Orlando, and since I still had my airline and hotel points from my previous work travels, I scheduled an interview and booked the trip.

Unfortunately, my interviewer canceled, so I wandered through the venue, handing out my resume during the day and partying at night.

On the last day of the show, I headed to the airport with no real prospects. I sat down at a bar as I waited for my flight. As it happened, the man beside me was a sales rep who had manned his company's booth at the show and was on his way home to Massachusetts.

Instinctually, I trusted him to watch my computer while I went to the bathroom, and, upon my return he introduced himself as Jerry.

Sales rep to sales rep, we chatted for about thirty minutes, and he was sympathetic to my corporate-buyout job loss. Before parting for our flight, he gave me his card and told me to give him a call, and maybe he could help me in the job market.

When I finally made it home, I collapsed into bed

and forgot all about the friendly, handsome guy Jerry at the bar who'd offered me a job lead. And the next morning, I woke up, drank my coffee, and watched the first plane hit the Twin Towers on the news. I couldn't believe it. Then, the second plane hit. The rest of the week was a blur as I watched the news with tears streaming down my face, reminding me of when I was six and saw John F. Kennedy assassinated on TV.

Jerry

Diana called me a few weeks after 9/11, asking if I had any job openings, and I told her she could come to a trade show in New York. I immediately let my boss know she was coming and that we might want to hire her, which we did.

When we'd met at the airport in Florida, I had been immediately attracted to her but tried not to show it because I didn't want our working relationship to be weird. We worked several other trade shows over the next months, and within a year, we were sharing an apartment in Rhode Island.

I had been married twice before, but I can honestly say that I had never been in love before I met Diana. She was different. I felt like God put her in my life because she honestly changed everything.

Diana

Jerry and I were soulmates, but like most couples, we'd had our share of problems, the most significant being our relationships with alcohol.

For me, drinking really began when I was fourteen. I grew up a preacher's kid in Tennessee and came from a very conservative home. My goal in life had been to "be a hippie," until I went to the airport with my parents one time—then I wanted to have a job where I traveled, walking through airports with a drink in one hand and a cigarette in the other.

Drinking began to take over my life, progressing through my teenage years, young adulthood, and into middle age. I made decisions based on my drinking—where to go, which hotels to stay in, and where to make appearances based on whether there was free booze.

When hangovers kept me from work, I knew just how much work I could miss, and then I would change jobs. I even chose alcohol over relationships.

When I started dating Jerry, I was the one who was always incapacitated by alcohol. Sometimes, Jerry would carry me home over his shoulder. We spent three or four years partying together, but ultimately, it was my behavior that set us on our journey of recovery.

I was so drunk and so beyond reasonable control, one day, Jerry carried me into the Crisis Center in New Bedford, MA, and put down the drink himself.

I spent five days in detox and then started going to Alcoholics Anonymous (AA) meetings after discharge, where I was struck with the idea that God could take away my obsession with drinking, and I thought, hey, that was enough. I thought that's all I needed—that I could do it without an AA sponsor, that God and I would do it all by ourselves.

It worked for eighteen months, for both me and Jerry. But sure enough, with only ourselves to fall back on, we relapsed, and I ended up right where I had been before, lying on a couch, drunk, a worthless piece of a human being.

Jerry was as fallen as I, relapsed, the both of us, if only for a day, and at that point we accepted that we needed to take the AA program seriously.

We got sponsors and did the "steps" in an AWOL (A Way of Life) group. We made new friends in AA that were active in the "outside world" and taught us how to have fun without alcohol, something that had been inconceivable to us before.

Finding God—a higher power—was and is essential in our permanent recovery. It was a matter of actually finding Him. As AA repeatedly taught us, "God never moved. You just have to look in the right places."

When we did look, sure enough He had not moved, and then, finding Him for certain, we both beat those demons. Both of us, together.

With an added bonus, sure now that together as a team we could overcome any challenge.

Then, four years into sobriety, the fire happened.

Light My Fire

Come on, baby, light my fire
Come on, baby, light my fire
Try to set the night on fire, yeah
—***Light My Fire*** *by The Doors*

<u>Diana</u>

Saturday, March 7, 2010, started out like any other day.

I sipped my coffee, staring out the windows of the sliding glass door into the backyard of our New Bedford, Massachusetts home. The disappointment and depression were becoming overwhelming. Losing my job after five years as an administrative assistant for a local building supply company hadn't been fun, but I understood. The construction market had crashed after the 2008-09 financial crisis, cutbacks had to be made, and people were losing their jobs left and right; it wasn't just me that was suffering. Still, it had been my "get-well job" after getting sober. That is to say, it was a job that I knew had to be local, without outside travel and the past temptations and potential relapses that could cause. Get well and stay well.

Now, my new plan was to go back to school, maybe get a degree in business, and give myself a solid shot at a new career. On the other hand, I had to admit to myself that, at fifty-four, it seemed foolish to waste time going to school instead of just looking for another job.

On top of that, it was less than a year since Jerry had broken off on his own and established his own janitorial/maintenance supply distributorship. It was he alone now, not a company above him—he was the company—pursuing contracts with manufacturers to distribute their products, while also lining up commercial client buyers. Jerry is a great salesman—extremely personable, people-loving, honest, enthusiastic, and a man of his word. When he promises a client anything, he delivers. Still, it was touch-and-go that first year, as is normal for a new business. As such, with Jerry then the primary bread-winner, and even that a bit shaky, I had to admit to a bit of guilt for my own lack of a job and my desire to delay that even longer with schooling.

That Saturday, it was still early morning, and my coffee downed, my thoughts were, *What to do now?* I'm a morning person, Jerry is the opposite. In the quiet house, there was nothing going on and it was too easy to wallow in negative emotions that came with these desperate jobless and uncertain-future thoughts, so I decided to do something I knew would make me feel better. Grabbing my keys and a bottle of suntan lotion, I headed out for the tanning salon.

An hour later, I ambled back into the house and noticed Jerry, finally awake, sitting at the kitchen table with his own cup of coffee in hand.

"What were you thinking about doing today?" I asked him.

"I was thinking we could go for a walk up by the cove. The weather is glorious. Seems like a shame to waste all this sunshine by staying inside."

I smiled at his suggestion. A walk around the fort by the ocean sounded wonderful, just what I needed to help pull me out of this funk. There's nothing I love more than being outside, enjoying the fresh air and sunshine. I had spent way too much time cooped up in the house during the horrible, hard winter we just experienced. After all, I was born and raised in the South, having lived there to my late thirties, and my body had never quite adjusted to the frigid, dreary New England winters compared to the mild winters of Tennessee. I was definitely ready for a day spent outdoors.

"That sounds perfect. When do you want to go?"

"Just let me finish my coffee and do my workout, then we can head that way."

I nodded at his response and started to plan out our route. If we walked the perimeter of Fort Taber and then headed over to the shoreline, our walk could take the better part of two hours. Satisfied with my plan, I grabbed myself a bottle of water and sat gazing out the sunroom's glass slider into the backyard while I waited for Jerry to be ready. Looking up at the sky, I asked myself, *What is my purpose... Why am I here, God?*

Thirty minutes later, my enthusiasm waned. I knew that Jerry was always serious about his workout, on the treadmill and equipment in the basement, but still, I was ready then.

Growing increasingly antsy and impatient, sitting around the house on such a beautiful day, once again those feelings of worthlessness were creeping back in as I sat in the silence of my own thoughts.

Determined to banish them, I stood from the table and strode purposefully out the back door.

Looking around my backyard oasis, I searched for something to do. The enormous ash tree growing in our backyard needed trimming. Its limbs had gone wild over the past year, and now they would block my sun when it finally got warm enough for me to lay out in the backyard and tan. Resolved to accomplish something useful and solve this problem, I grabbed a hacksaw and a stepladder, then set to work.

About forty-five minutes later, the sound of Jerry's irritated voice interrupted my efforts. "What the heck are you doing, Diana?"

My shoulders tensed at his tone. Here I was, trying to be useful, and instead of being appreciative, he was out here scolding me like a child. Of course, maybe that's how he was beginning to see me the longer I remained unemployed and couldn't figure out what to do with my life.

"These limbs were going to be blocking my sun. I just wanted to get them trimmed real quick. I'd hoped to be done by the time you were ready."

"Fine, climb down from there and give me the saw. I'll get this finished up so we can go for a walk."

[*Aside from Jerry: Diana wasn't really good at finishing what she started, especially things she wasn't qualified to handle, such as using a hacksaw to cut tree limbs. So, this wasn't in any way unusual.*]

Grumbling to myself over his sour disposition, I climbed down from the ladder, then began gathering the branches I had already cut and stuffing them into the chiminea by the patio.

Jerry being Jerry, with his own sizable obsessive-compulsive disorder (OCD) he could not let the incomplete trimming stand, and he got to work trimming the branches more extensively, properly, getting the bigger stuff that I couldn't.

By the time Jerry had finished the actual trimming, it was late afternoon and his mild irritation had become more pronounced. "Let's just get this lit and burned," he groused. "There's no way it will be done burning in time for us to go for a walk, but at least we can have dinner on time."

[*Aside from Jerry: Something to look forward to, always, Diana's cooking. Southern in particular, with a Northern twist on the veggies.*]

I was just as ready to be done with the project—and his attitude—so I quickly retrieved the lighter fluid and doused the limbs. Jerry's first attempt to light the fire was unsuccessful, as were his second and third. After emptying the entire can of lighter fluid onto the green wood, we still couldn't get it to ignite. Fed up with the whole situation—and again, with his OCD, not one to leave a job undone—Jerry retrieved from the shed the gas can we used for filling our lawn equipment and he poured it over the branches.

Before he could even strike a match to get the fire started, the gasoline fumes combusted from whatever tiny ember was hidden in the bundle. Flames exploded out the sides of the chiminea's metal grate and shot out the top in a fiery burst that reached well above the roof of our house.

It's almost certain that I would have caught fire no matter what, considering my extreme proximity to the chiminea at the time of the explosion, but the sweats I was wearing—soaked in tanning oil as they were—meant that I was quickly engulfed in a fire so hot that the flames burned blue and white.

Panic engulfed me as quickly as the flames, but strangely, I felt no pain. Looking down at my body, I could see fire everywhere. *I needed to stop, drop, and roll*, I thought in a panicked daze, but the ground around me appeared to be on fire, too. Surely rolling around in flames would only make things worse, wouldn't it? Determined to find a spot that wasn't burning, I ran towards the front yard and onto our driveway. No matter where I went, looking down to see my way, everything around me was still in flames. *How did the fire spread so fast? How am I going to put myself out if everything is on fire?*

Jerry appeared through the flames and tried to push me to the ground. *What is he doing?* I wondered. *Didn't he realize the ground was on fire, too?*

Suddenly, Jerry's shouting broke through the haze of my panic. "Put out Diana! Put out Diana!"

As it had so happened, our next-door neighbor, Corey, had come out after seeing the explosion and was spraying down our burning fence and awnings with his garden hose. *Crap, Jerry's gonna be pissed about me catching all that on fire*, I thought without reason. In fact, at Jerry's call "Put out Diana", Corey had immediately turned the garden hose on me and doused the flames that covered me.

Once the fire was finally out, I got my panic somewhat under control. "Can you just pour the water on my head?" I asked Corey. I didn't know why, but I just really wanted him to soak my head in water.

I saw that Jerry was on the phone with 911 and that our neighbors were gathering around me, some holding blankets, some just staring in shock and horror. *This is all my fault,* I thought miserably. *Jerry wanted to go for a nice walk, and instead I just had to get that tree trimmed today. Today! And now his whole day is going to be ruined by having to deal with my nonsense.*

As the sirens drew nearer, I asked Corey to turn the hose on the chiminea, which was still burning. I feared that because it was so close to the propane tank on the grill, if that blew up, it was the end of everything in the backyard and more.

Jerry knelt beside me.

"Jer, I think I'm a dead duck this time," I confided.

"You can't die," he insisted. "Because I can't live without you." His firm words held a confidence and conviction that let me know that giving up was not an option. I was ashamed of the foolishness that led to this moment, and afraid about what the extent of my injuries might be, but I knew from the look on his face that I had to do everything I could to survive if for no other reason than because I loved him and owed it to him to try.

Finally, the EMTs arrived. "Ma'am, do you think you can stand up on your own?" one of them asked.

"I think so," I replied, and I did.

"Great, that's great," he said. "Now, do you think you can put yourself on the stretcher?"

"I think so," I repeated, and once again, I did.

"You're doing great," he told me as he and his partner loaded the stretcher into the back of the ambulance. "Now we're going to give you this shot of fentanyl, and we'll get you to the hospital and patched up in no time." They acted and spoke positively, reassuringly, but the look on their faces told me otherwise.

I nodded mutely as the Fentanyl took effect, and my world went dark.

(It would be many months later that I would learn that I should have stopped, dropped, and rolled, because the ground was <u>not</u> on fire. That I had simply seen it as burning flames, as my hair was on fire and when I would look down it would flop in front of my view, and that's what I was seeing, those flames.)

Jerry

I hadn't anticipated cutting branches that morning. I had shut off the water at the valve in the basement and stored the hoses in the shed out back for winter.

[*Aside from Diana: That's the OCD part of Jerry that I love. Neat. Orderly.*]

Had I known we would burn branches that day, I would've had all that stuff set up.

[*Aside from Diana: He would have. OCD again, the good part.*]

The chimenea itself wasn't really big enough to burn wood, and there we were trying to burn these big green branches.

It irritated me that the morning wasn't going as expected, and I wasn't thinking clearly. Nothing could have been more stupid than adding gas to the fire—but that's exactly what I did. Gas isn't a good accelerant because the liquid doesn't burn, but the vapors combust and explode. That's exactly what happened; I was literally pouring the gas when everything exploded. I should have been the one burned. But when the flash hit her, she ignited like a tiki torch, burning clear flames.

I felt helpless trying to extinguish her. The skin melted off my hands the second I touched her, but I never felt it because I was so worried about her. It was my responsibility as the man to protect my woman, and I just couldn't do it.

[*Aside from Diana: Later on, when Jerry would be expressing to my Mom his feelings of guilt, my sweet Mom would try and console him with "Diana has always been accident prone," though that could never erase the image of that gas can in hand.*]

Never had I felt so helpless in all my life—never. Briefly, I considered jumping on her to force her to drop and roll, but that would only have set me on fire without helping her at all.

After our neighbor finally put her out, she sat there smoking in the driveway.

[*Aside from Diana: My original idea for this book's title was "The Day I Quit Smoking."*]

Neighbors came over with blankets. I dialed 911, and the flesh from my fingers came off and stuck to the phone. The skin was hanging off my hands like wax on a melted candle. The emergency operator was asking all kinds of questions, and I just kept reciting the address and saying, "Get over here. We need somebody here. There's a severe burn injury. People are hurt." And I wasn't answering any of their questions, just saying the address over and over.

After I hung up, I looked down at her, and she looked up at me.

"I can't survive this," she told me.

My heart broke.

"You have to," I told her. "Because I can't live without you."

The next thing I knew, the EMTs were there, trying to get me into an ambulance. I don't know if I was in some kind of shock or what, but I fought with them. I just wanted to make sure that they took care of Diana.

They got mad at me. "Sir, if you don't come with us, you will lose your hand."

"I don't care," I told them. "I don't care if I lose my arms. Don't worry about me—just take care of her."

They didn't fight with me anymore. After the EMTs had loaded Diana up and left, others came back over to me. "Are you going to let us take care of you now?"

"Yeah," I said.

They got me in the ambulance and gave me a shot of fentanyl.

You hear about fentanyl in the news. It's supposed to be the bad stuff. But I've got to tell you, it ain't bad stuff when you're in pain, and I was really feeling the pain in my hands then. They could have told me they wanted to amputate both my legs and arms, and I would have said, "Go ahead." It was a total transformation.

Without the pain, I became totally fixated on Diana. She was all I talked about.

"You hear that noise," one EMT told me as we arrived at St. Luke's Hospital. "That's the rotors of the chopper leaving the top of the building on its way to Mass General Hospital in Boston." They told me that St. Luke's didn't have burn capabilities, and that she was going to the best place to get treated.

When they stopped at St. Luke's, they didn't even take me out of the ambulance. The driver went in for a moment, then they drove me to Mass General Hospital, too. At that moment, I felt calmer. I don't know if it was the fentanyl or the fact that Diana was probably landing at the best hospital to help her, or that I was heading to that same hospital right then, and I would see her again soon.

She had to be all right.

She was my angel.

Still Smoldering

> *When I'm at my weakest*
> *I will trust in Jesus*
> *Always in the highs and lows*
> *The One who goes before me*
> *God is in this story*
> —***God Is in This Story*** *by Big Daddy Weave and*
> *Katy Nichole*

<u>Diana</u>

I woke suddenly to find myself lying in a hammock. Somehow, I had gotten tangled in it and couldn't escape. Searing pain and heat made me realize someone had suspended me above a large cooking fire.

"Help!" I screamed, as my limbs flailed uselessly around me. "Please, somebody, help!"

As my eyes bounced around the room in search of rescue, I saw I was in a tent filled with people attending a family gathering. Not one of them paused in their conversations to even glance at me. It was like I was invisible; like I wasn't even there.

Am I dead? Is this hell? I wondered.

Gradually, I noticed voices coming from outside the tent. I strained to hear what they were saying. As the sounds became clearer, I realized they were talking about me. Hope flared to life in my chest, only to be extinguished as I picked up on the negative, somber tone of their discussion. It seemed they wanted to help me, but they didn't believe they could.

Are they giving up? Are they just going to leave me here, roasting over this fire forever?

Suddenly, Jerry's voice joined the conversation.

Finally, I thought, overjoyed at his arrival. *Help is here.*

I knew there was no way Jerry could see my suffering and not do something. Just as quickly as relief set in, it evaporated. Jerry was angry with me, and he wasn't going to help.

Why? What had I done to him that he would abandon me like this?

As I searched my mind, the revelation came: *the fire*. It had been my fault. I'd ruined everything. Of course, he wasn't going to help me; he was probably glad to be rid of me.

Diana

The second I arrived at Mass General, they stuck me in the ICU and doped me up on pain meds and psych drugs, which prevented me from remembering any of what really happened while simultaneously inducing wild hallucinations. Even the respiratory therapist who tended to me at St. Luke's said that I was talking to her the whole time like nothing was wrong, though I remember none of that.

For three months, my life was a collage of hallucinations and dreams. Consciously, I didn't have a clue what was really going on around me. Unconsciously, I was surviving.

[*Aside from Jerry: During those months with her completely out of it, I was talking to her all the time to subliminally help her survive, knowing that somehow she was hearing me and would do the rest, fight hard to survive.*]

Jerry

When I arrived at Mass General, they didn't have any rooms available in the burn ward, so they created a private space for me right there in the Emergency room behind curtains. Despite the concerns of my doctors as to my own condition, I didn't have room to worry about myself while my mind raced with concern for Diana, replaying the events of the past few hours over and over. Guilt took up almost as much space in my brain as worry. I had thrown the gasoline that caused the explosion of flames. It was my fault—no doubt about it.

Images of our life together—our humble home, our two cats, our simple daily routines—flashed through my mind like a movie reel as I wondered if I'd ever experience any of it again. Was I about to lose my soulmate to my own recklessness? Trying to imagine what life might be like if I lost her was just too painful. There is no me without Diana.

Even as I spiraled deeper, Diana's voice crept into my mind. I could imagine what she'd say if she were there with me. *Cut the drama, Jer. I'll be fine.*

The imagined words brought me back to the present. *Who would care for the cats while we were in the hospital* I wondered, trying to refocus my mind on the more immediate issues within my control. *How will I notify our friends and family?* The skin had melted off my hands, so it wasn't like I could pick up the phone and call them.

Suddenly, I heard a familiar voice from the other side of the curtain. "Well, how many people named Laperriere could you have in here?"

Tony, my friend from work, was in the hospital with his son, who had a leg infection. Despite my gruesome appearance and chaotic emotional state, I was glad to see him. His quick visit took my mind off worrying about Diana for a minute. I still don't know how he learned I was in the hospital that day, but God puts people just where and when you need them.

Later that evening, I was moved to the burn unit—Bigelow 13—which was on the same floor as the ICU where Diana was being treated. I continued to probe the doctors and nurses for an update on her condition, but they were all tight-lipped.

That can't be a good sign.

I would cling to hope when they told me, "She's in the right place."

Unfortunately, most of the explanations about her condition included things like:

"She is very, very ill."

"Her condition is very serious."

"Her injuries are critical."

Their vague responses and negative demeanor frustrated me. What they didn't tell me then but that I soon enough learn was that most all burn patients her age did not survive. As well, most patients, no matter their age, with burns so severe usually died from infection.

Eventually, they sedated me, which was probably for the best. I was in shock, and while my concern for Diana was pushing the pain from my thoughts, it was also keeping me from resting. Severe burns come with a high chance of infection, so they took me to surgery almost immediately to graft skin from my thigh onto my left hand and onto a spot on my right shin where my pants had caught fire.

After I woke up from anesthesia, I had the pleasure of meeting my roommate, who was an absolute nut job. Shouting and vulgar language poured from his mouth day and night, and the painkillers weren't enough to let me pass out and ignore it all.

On the third evening, I woke to find him standing alongside my bed, staring down at me. In no uncertain terms, I told him that for his own safety, he should return to his bed before I inflicted a beating on him. The next day, they moved me to another room, where I stayed for a day or two by myself before I met new roommates who were much more pleasant.

One of the attending doctors for the burn unit, Dr. Colleen Ryan, checked in with me. She was very nice, making sure that I had everything I needed. All I wanted was information about Diana, but her responses were then vague, carefully worded.

Dr. Ryan would eventually become our bedrock in the hospital, and I honestly don't think I would have survived without her. She was a skilled surgeon, but as importantly she was also compassionate and a genuine saint of a human being.

Laura Bridges was a counselor who would also stop by to ask about my emotional well-being, how I felt overall, and if I needed to talk about what happened. Truthfully, I wasn't sure how I felt. I missed talking with Diana. Guilt consumed me. Because of my hasty carelessness—really, dumping gasoline to get a fire burning?—the person who meant the most to me was lying in a nearby ICU fighting for her life. Laura was friendly and compassionate, and she helped me deal with my feelings.

As I lay there—groggy on pain medication—many friends and family passed through to visit, but I don't remember any of that. I found out long later that Diana's Mom, Virginia, had come all the way from Tennessee. Yvonne, Diana's best friend there—more like a sister—was Mom's rock in this sudden, unexpected tragedy, and arranged everything and flew in with Mom. Even more, Yvonne gave Mom the moral support that at the age of 78 she needed.

Mostly, I remember my world being dark. I felt useless. Friends told me I appeared to be sleepwalking through life, but inside I found it hard to see any hint of a bright future on the horizon. What future?

I cried when no one was around and especially when I spoke of the accident to others. Sometimes, I would close my eyes and pray for Diana until I fell asleep. But sleep was not an escape from my dark thoughts as I relived the accident over and over. I truly believe this was the lowest point in my life.

On day four, they let me see Diana. I was afraid, uncertain of what I might encounter. My stomach flip-flopped, my body trembled, and I felt lightheaded. When I entered the burn ICU, my gaze immediately caught on the sheets of plastic surrounding each bed. The beeps, buzzes, and chimes of medical equipment surrounded Diana's motionless form. Encased as she was in bandages, she looked more like a mummy than my Diana. I asked the nurse if she had lost any body parts, and they told me she might lose her ears and the end of her nose.

There were photos taped to the wall, pictures of Diana, me, and our families and friends. They had been brought by Diana's mom and local friends in order to humanize Diana to the caregivers, making her more than just another patient or number. I would later gather more items to display.

Diana didn't show any sign that she knew I was there, but I started speaking to her anyway, telling her how much she meant to me, how much I loved her, how strong she was. I had to convince her, I felt, to come back to me, that I was lost without her, that I was there then and would always be there beside her.

I returned to my room teary-eyed, asking God to get us through this ordeal. I hoped and prayed that we would again enjoy life together. And the feelings of guilt, fear, and helplessness returned in full force.

Since the moment Diana arrived at the hospital, Dr. Fagan, the burn ward team leader, had worked feverishly to source skin for her in order to avoid infection. Her surgeons, Drs. Goverman, Ryan, and Sheridan, initially covered her body with cadaver and pig skin, but ultimately, the body will only accept its own skin permanently. They took skin from her head, belly, and buttocks, but it was difficult because she had third-degree burns on ninety percent of her body, which required grafts. They also began growing cultured skin from the cells taken from her body.

The feedback on Diana's recovery was mixed, and none of it was great. The survival formula they used at the time Diana was burned gave her a negative forty percent chance of making it—her age minus the size of her burn. That is, a _negative_ forty percent chance. Not a fifty percent chance. Not a ten percent chance. Not a one percent chance. A negative forty percent chance. A minus-forty percent chance.

During Diana's initial time in the burn ICU, at least four patients there—their burns were not as extensive and severe as Diana's—died, did not make it. A reason that Diana didn't initially die early on, we figure, is because while on fire she did not scream. So, she did not have inhalation injuries. Her lungs had not been burned inside. That is what saved her, her not screaming, not sucking in flames.

No one wanted to give false hope, but the lack of optimism really crushed me. I was told a number of times by the staff, quietly, that Diana was the worst one they'd ever seen.

During those first days, the doctor who admitted me to the emergency room and one of the nurses had expressed to me very negative outlooks, believing she would not survive, or, on the off chance that she did, her quality of life would be dreadful.

They seemed to be waiting for her to get an infection, which some believed was the most likely outcome. All I wanted was a glimmer of hope, but no one would give that to me.

By day six, I still didn't know much. I said the Lord's Prayer every day and prayed that God would restore our lives to functionality. The most positive thing was that Diana hadn't gotten an infection during that first week—much to the surprise of the entire care team. Still, there was a lot of negative energy around her, and I honestly had no idea if she would survive.

On day seven, they discharged me from the hospital, and a friend of mine, Mark Boulay, took me home. Though I didn't want to leave Diana, I was definitely ready to leave the hospital. As the medical staff took me downstairs in a wheelchair, anxiety and uncertainty about returning to the scene of the accident filled me. Mark pulled his truck up to the front door of the hospital. Bandages covered the burns on my left hand and right shin, as well as my left thigh, where they had taken skin for my graft.

Intense pain, both from the graft and the uncertainty in my heart, made it hard to act tough. Dressed in sheets and blankets—my clothes had been burned beyond recognition and discarded—I figured I probably looked as fragile as I felt.

As we drew closer to our house, I began to worry about the state I would find it in. Mark told me I needed to pull it together, to be strong for Diana, but everything felt so overwhelming.

My eyes grew wide as we pulled into the driveway. The fire had melted the fence, singed the awnings, and discolored the sunroom. When I looked at the yard, all I saw was a reenactment of that day. The container of gas still sat beside the chimenea, almost accusing me. The melted garbage cans sat abandoned near the gas grill cover, which had burned right through to where the propane container sat. How close had that come to exploding and killing us all?

Inside, the house smelled like a kennel. The cats were traumatized and had pooped everywhere. My sister, Jeannine, had helped out, feeding the cats and emptying the litter box, but I could see it would need a lot of work to restore the cleanliness that I needed. [*Aside from Diana: Remember that OCD of his?*]

At first, I was upset, but Mark set me straight by praising those who had done their best to help. Exhaustion overwhelmed me as we said our goodbyes, so I took my medications and went to bed, but got little rest in the end. Instead, horrific nightmares assaulted me all night long.

Hills and Valleys

On the mountains, I will bow my life
To the One who set me there
In the valley, I will lift my eyes to the One who sees me there
When I'm standing on the mountain, I didn't get there on my own
When I'm walking through the valley, I know I am not alone
You're God of the hills and valleys
*—**Hills and Valleys** by Tauren Wells*

Jerry

The day after I arrived home, Mark returned to help me haul off the yard waste from the fire. We gathered up all the debris, melted pots, and charred plants, then tossed it all into the back of his truck so we could take it to the dump.

"What do you want to do with the chiminea?" Mark asked.

"Just get rid of it," I replied. "I never want to see that damned thing again."

I spent the rest of the afternoon scrubbing the outside of the house with graffiti remover to get rid of the smoke residue and replacing the gutter shields that had melted in the sunroom.

My hands were still wrapped, which made the job even harder than it should have been, and I probably should have been resting, but my need to take care of the house wouldn't let me. I wanted to collapse in exhaustion by the time I'd finished, but my own needs and comfort wasn't an option. Instead, I showered, called on a few client accounts, and then headed back to Boston to visit Diana.

"How is she?" I asked the nurses once I'd arrived. Their answers were the same as always—vague, and with a realistic and negative undertone.

Turning to look into the room, I saw the nurses dressing her wounds, revealing the incredible amount of damage her body had suffered. Grief sought to overwhelm me, but I beat it back. *I won't cry here. Not in front of her.* It wasn't some macho need to appear too tough for tears that had me fighting back the moisture building in my eyes; it was Diana. Everyone around her was so negative, so sure that she wouldn't make it, and I refused to be a part of that negativity.

To me, she was going to live. She had to. I wouldn't survive if she didn't, and I knew she needed all the positivity and encouragement she could get, so I blinked back my tears, then headed into the room to sit at her side and tell her about my day.

"You know she can't hear you, don't you?" the nurse said.

"Yes, she can," I argued. "She may not know what I'm saying, but she can hear my voice. She knows I'm here and I haven't given up on her. My voice here, talking to her every day, will make sure she knows that there is someone waiting for her and she has a reason to fight and get better."

As soon as the nurse left the room, taking her negative attitude with her, I prayed out loud, using the same prayer that had helped me through the grief of losing my mother the previous November, and it comforted me, just as it had then. I knew that whatever might come, God was with us.

This became a pattern—long, agonizing days split between cleaning and repairing our home, taking care of our cats, and calling on distributors to keep my business afloat. I had sales accounts throughout New England in Massachusetts, Rhode Island, Connecticut, Vermont, New Hampshire, and Maine. All this made my schedule and ability to visit Diana erratic and unpredictable, but I was determined not to let that stop me.

Whether it was early in the morning before work, or ten at night, I went to Mass General to visit her every single day. I was so grateful to the staff who understood my determination to spend time with her daily and would let me come well before or well passed the permitted visiting hours. On the weekends, I made a point of bringing with me her friends or the pastor from our church for visits so that she would know that I wasn't the only one waiting for her to come home. The schedule was exhausting, but I saw so many patients in that burn ward who never had anyone visit them, and they didn't make it. I was determined that Diana would have all the support and encouragement I could offer.

Diana

"Stop, DEA!" I shouted at the drug dealers I was chasing through the university campus.

My legs pumped, eating up the ground beneath me, but the criminals continued to flee. The distance between us grew larger until they abruptly changed course to cut across the street and duck into a theater.

Bursting through the doors, I quickly scanned the crowd and realized I'd lost them. Frustration welled up—right alongside a sudden urge to use the restroom. I darted toward the sign for the ladies' room, but my foot slipped on a program someone had dropped. Efforts to regain my footing were useless as I continued to slip on the carpet of papers theater patrons seemed to have left scattered all over the lobby's floor.

Just as I crashed into a heap on the floor, frustrated and ready to scream, an "Employees Only" door opened, and a woman emerged and headed straight toward me.

"I live here, and you are not my patient, but I'll help you anyway," she announced.

Suddenly, she was forcing me to my side and shoving my face into bars that had appeared out of nowhere beside me. Claustrophobia set in as agonizing pain shot through my body.

"Hurry, please hurry," I begged as my breath came in short, hysterical pants. *Panic attack*, some remote part of my brain supplied. *I'm having a panic attack.* Dark spots danced across my vision as I fought for air and continued to beg the woman—who I finally realized was a nurse—to finish changing my diaper quickly and free me from the agony of her touch and the panic of having my face forced up against the hospital bed's rails.

Jerry

About a week after I came home from the hospital, my son Scott called.

"Dad, I have nowhere to go."

He was broke, and he needed a place to stay while he got back on his feet.

I raised Scott after my divorce. I knew he had been struggling, but I was struggling too, trying to keep everything together, pay the bills, and be there for Diana.

The two people who were most important in my life needed me.

Days morphed into weeks and then months. Between working, visiting Diana, and helping Scott, I found myself sleepwalking through life. I even put my own burn recovery on the back burner, so much so that I completely forgot to get the staples in my leg removed. The pain of their removal when they were pulled out weeks later paled in comparison to the deep emotional pain I suffered as each new day passed without Diana waking up or Scott's situation getting better.

Diana and I had both been active in AA before the fire, and while I can't say I'm grateful for all we went through with our drinking, I was tremendously grateful for the skills I learned in that program, which helped me as I took Diana's burn recovery one day at a time. The support and prayers of my friends—both in and out of AA—made a tremendous difference in my ability to keep hoping and praying.

With Diana, the initial reprieve from infection lasted ninety days—a miracle—but when it ended, it tested my faith. Her fever spiked so high that the medical staff would have to pump her full of new drugs, killing off the infection only for another infection to pop up in its place.

This stressful cycle of peaks and valleys continued for months until one day, one of her doctors asked me to come speak with him in his office.

"You know she's never going to walk again," he said. "She'll never feed herself, never use her arms and legs, never be able to bathe herself. Her quality of life is going to be non-existent. She'll require fulltime home nursing care 24/7." He paused, then added, "So, maybe next time she gets an infection…..perhaps we should think about comfort measures instead of treatment."

Horror overwhelmed me. *He wants me to let her die*, I realized. Finally, fury washed away the horror. "What did you just say? Don't ever call me in here to tell me that again." [*Aside from Diana: Watch it, Doc! Don't poke the bear.*]

I stormed out of his office and down to the parking lot, unwilling to take my negative attitude into Diana's hospital room. Unable to get my emotions under control even as I drove home, I called Dr. Colleen Ryan, always dependable and reassuring—someone I completely trusted.

"He's a good doctor, Jerry," she told me. "Serving in the military—triaging soldiers on the battlefield, he was choosing who lives or dies based on who is more likely to survive. And it has made him look at things differently."

While her answer explained his attitude and words, it did nothing to appease the storm of my emotions. *Was Diana going to die? Was I selfishly prolonging her suffering by insisting on all this treatment?* The thought horrified me even more than the doctor's words had, and for the first time since the accident, I felt genuine despair.

As I drove through a tunnel, I heard a voice say, *"Who are you to doubt me?"* And I didn't doubt again after that. I just believed that God was on our side and was sternly reminded that life is a gift.

Dr. Ryan herself would prove to a part of that gift. She made me feel that I could talk to her about anything any time.

During the many months of Diana's time in Mass General, Dr. Ryan was a spirit uplifter. She wasn't one to offer false hope, but she continually encouraged me with her own positive advice. "Don't give up hope, Jerry," she often told me. And, "She's behaving like a survivor." With her years treating burn patients, Dr. Ryan would know their behaviors, positive and negative, and hearing her encouraging words so often boosted and helped me maintain my own optimism.

[*Aside from Diana: Not to downplay or overlook Dr. Ryan's surgical skills and attention to detail. She is the reason that I still have eyelashes and breast tissue.*]

Diana

As the boat reached the dock of the sub-basement river, I looked around in amazement at the life-size arcade game. At ten stories high, the game had everything. I had to pass through dens of drug dealing, prostitution, and drinking on the lower levels in order to make it to the luxurious spa at the top.

I tried, again and again, to defeat the levels and earn my prize of being pampered, but I continued to fail over and over. My efforts did not go unnoticed, however, and one day the game's owner approached me.

"Diana, I've seen you here a lot recently," he said. "Your tenacity and creativity are impressive. To be honest, we haven't been doing well financially, and I'm worried I won't be able to keep this place open much longer."

"Oh no, this place is wonderful!" My heart sank. Visiting the game had been a blast, and I'd hate for it to close before I got the chance to visit the spa.

"I'm glad to hear you feel that way. How would you like to be the general manager of the facility?"

My eyebrows rose in surprise. "Wow, that's amazing. What are the benefits?"

The owner listed out an impressive compensation package, including unlimited spa services during my off hours. I was sold.

The learning curve was steep, and at first, I wasn't sure I could do it.

The more I dove into the operations of things, the more I saw how complex the entire system was. *No wonder this place was struggling.* There were just so many moving parts.

Eventually, though, I got the hang of things, and instead of feeling like I was treading water just to keep afloat, I began to feel like I was thriving.

Starting off my shift one day on the casino floor, I began circulating amongst the tables. A sudden burst of uproarious laughter from a nearby group caught my attention, and I headed over to see what had attracted the gathered crowd.

A man in a white hat stood at the center of the group, telling jokes and charming everyone. *Jerry*, I realized. I wasn't sure how I knew him or if he knew me, but I knew who he was, and I knew I loved him.

[*Aside from Jerry: Nice to see Diana acknowledging my humor; usually she'll just roll her eyes. Not that she hasn't heard the same jokes over and over a thousand times.*]

Jerry

After about two months, I entered the ICU, and Diana could speak to me for the first time—nothing more than some delusional chatter, but I saw it as progress.

Peaks.

Shortly afterward, she fell into another bout with infection and almost died.

Valleys.

Every day during my visit, I sang to her as well. The nurses thought it was cute, but that's because they didn't understand what I was doing. Diana hated my singing—I can't sing a lick—and I knew eventually she would wake up and tell me I couldn't sing. I made up my own version of Sonny and Cher's "All I Ever Need Is You" to torment her into opening her eyes and telling me to stop.

Finally, one day she woke and was aware enough to know who I was. She looked right at me and said, "I love you, but you know you can't sing, right?"

I looked at the nurses who heard what Diana had just said and laughed at the amazed look on their faces.

I know my girl.

Higher Level of Consciousness

When I was just a girl
I thought I had it figured out
See, my life would turn out right
And I'd make it here somehow
But things don't always come that easy
And sometimes I would doubt
—***Free to Be** Me by Francesca Battistelli*

<u>Diana</u>

The day I woke up was terrifying and disorienting. Between the muscle and nerve damage caused by the burns and the encasement of all the bandages, I couldn't move much more than my eyes. All I knew was that I was alive, in really bad shape, and Jerry wasn't there. As those realizations sank in, I started sobbing.

"Why are you crying?" asked a nurse.

"Jerry doesn't love me anymore. He's not here," I told her.

"Jerry's been here every day."

I sniffled. "Is he here now?"

"No, but he should be here any minute."

As the minutes passed, every male I saw through the vision-blurring plastic had me crying out, "Jerry, are you there?"

The nurses would come over and tell me, "He's not here yet, Diana, but he'll be here."

Their reassurances didn't stop me, though, and I kept calling for him until finally—there he was—and I felt a warm, safe glow. He was here, he still loved me, and he would not leave me.

He smiled, then settled in for what I learned was his daily visit. Instead of singing and talking to me, we watched the New England Patriots football game on the little television in my bubble. As I relaxed, the scene shifted, and suddenly we were in a bar with plastic tarps hanging because of construction. Bartenders in hospital scrubs rolled drink carts in between the plastic sheets, and I bargained with one of them for swabs moistened with water, and she agreed to give me one every fifteen minutes.

And every five minutes, I would ask, "Can I have another?", which made her more irritated, insisting that she would watch the time and give me a moist swab every fifteen minutes.

That didn't stop me, though. "Has it been fifteen

minutes yet?" I kept asking.

Finally fed up, she told me I wasn't her only customer and walked off. I wondered who was picking up the tab for all these swabs. Hopefully, Jerry, since I didn't think I had my purse. I kept the used swabs and pestered Jerry to dip them in his bottled water in between the new swabs. I was so thirsty, and I couldn't understand why the bartenders were being so stingy with the swabs. *Isn't it their job to sell drinks?* I wondered. I could tell Jerry felt guilty for being my accomplice, but he did what I wanted him to do. He kept telling me they would kick him out, but that didn't make any sense. *Why would they kick him out of the bar for giving me swabs?*

Jerry

"Hey, Mom Tenney," I greeted my mother-in-law calling from Tennessee.

Well, not my actual mother-in-law. Diana and I had marriage plans before the burn, but, as with so many other things, the fire derailed those arrangements for the time being. Now, our guest list sat abandoned in Diana's planner, and her wedding dress languished in her closet, wrapped in a garment bag and nearly forgotten.

Tragedy has a way of reminding a man that life is short. Diana brightened my days, and I missed her so much; I was broken without her. As soon as she was able, I was determined to make her my wife.

"How's my girl today?" Mom Tenney asked.

"Really great, actually. We watched another Pats game together. I'm so glad she's staying lucid for longer periods of time. One of her doctors told me today that she is the strongest person he has ever seen come through the burn unit. Her survival so far has been nothing short of a miracle, and they told me if she can make it to Spaulding Rehabilitation Hospital, she should be more or less out of the woods."

"That's wonderful! I know life will never be the same for the two of you, but I am so glad she has you to walk with her through all this."

The words warmed my heart. I knew she was right. The road to recovery would be long, but I was prepared to take that journey with Diana, to be by her side every step of the way. I asked for prayers for her from everyone in our church each Sunday, as well as during every AA meeting I attended. Those were the places I went for comfort and hope. Even though we had the goal of eventually making it to Spaulding Rehab in sight, we were still very much in a season of peaks and valleys.

Spontaneous fevers still occasionally plagued Diana,

and one day while she was in a high fever state, she kept calling me 'Mark'.

"Don't you recognize me, sweetie? It's Jerry," I told her.

"I see Mark," she said.

Later, we found out that Mark — a truck driver friend of ours who had gone missing — had pulled over in a rest area and had a heart attack in his sleeper cab. This wasn't the only time Diana seemed to talk to someone who had recently departed, and each incident made me fear she was standing closer to Heaven's gate than I was ready for her to be. During this season of waiting, I leaned on God, on prayer, on family, and friends as the only things that could bring us through.

Diana

At the sight of the nurses with their rolls of gauze entering the room, I began to hyperventilate. My chest tightened and my vision narrowed as tears streamed down my face and the familiar feeling of a panic attack set in. After months of being in and out of surgeries, having repeated renal failure, and needing nitroglycerin administered twice to restart my heart — the thing that still terrified me the most was having my bandages changed.

The process took place daily, and it lasted for three hours. The feeling of people touching me was excruciating all by itself, but add in having to be moved around and hoisted in the Hoyer, (a contraption hung over me like a hoist to lift an engine from a car), and the entire experience became intolerable.

"We can't give you any more pain meds," the nurse informed me matter-of-factly, just as she did every day. I knew she was just doing her job, but her lack of compassion in the face of my obvious suffering made the awful experience even worse. I wasn't oblivious to the fact that neither she nor any of my other nurses thought I would make it. The way I looked at it through my individual suffering was that they all thought the time spent on my care—the extraordinary amount of energy and resources that went into my daily bandage changing and everything else I needed—was taking away their attention from patients who had a real shot at survival. It made me wonder why I should have to endure the process.

By the time Jerry arrived that evening, I'd had enough. "Please, just take me home," I begged him.

"Diana, you know I love you, and I wish you were at home with me, but there's no way I can give you the care you need right now. As soon as you're able, I promise, I promise, I'll take you home." My heart sank at his refusal. I couldn't do it anymore, I just couldn't.

"Jer, I'm going to die either way. Can't I just do it at home? Can I have the peace and comfort of being with you instead of being tortured with all the surgeries and bandaging and everything else they do to me here?"

A look of outrage overtook Jerry's face. "Who said you're going to die? You tell me who said that right now."

It was typical of Jerry to go straight into protective mode instead of focusing on what I was asking of him. I loved that about him, but right then I also just wanted to go home. "No one said that, Jer, but I can tell. They think working on me is a waste of time."

Jerry

The instant I left Diana's room, I went straight to Dr. Fagan about the nurses' attitudes. I'd been so careful to keep my discouragement away from her, and I'd already gone toe-to-toe with one of her surgeons over his attitude toward her chances of survival. There was no way I was going to let some nurses undermine her confidence and belief in her own recovery.

The very next day, they assigned Edna to Diana.

Oh, what a blessing. That woman was a saint, a ray of sunshine that burst into our lives in the dreary space of that hospital and breathed new life into me and

Diana. Edna was so much a booster of Diana's spirits, so essential to her recovery. Just a week after Edna started tending to Diana, I came in to find her painting Diana's fingernails blue.

"They let you do nail polish during your shift?" I asked. "Those other nurses acted like they barely had time to take care of Diana."

Edna chuckled good-naturedly. "Oh no, I definitely don't have time to paint nails during my shift, but I got off half an hour ago. I just know how much Diana likes her nails done, so I thought I'd stay a little late today and do them for her."

[*Aside from Diana: This was another time of those half-reality/half-hallucination situations, when I must have been going into an infection. Yes, Edna was doing my nails, but I was seeing it as happening in Jerry's sister's trailer and Edna had come over to do them.*]

The kind, unexpected gesture warmed my heart. How was it that this woman, after a twelve-hour shift, would give freely of her own time to do something so small yet so important as to help my Diana feel more beautiful?

It's remarkable how God sends us angels in times of tribulation to remind us of his grace and goodness. I truly believe that is what Edna was for us.

Diana

"Diana, I just wanted to say I'm sorry." The nurse addressing me was one of those who had been reassigned away from me for her negative attitude. Despite the discouragement I had experienced, I didn't bear any of them any ill will. It can't be easy to spend your career working with people who have such grim chances of survival, and it was nice of her to stop by and say she'd been wrong.

There had certainly been some bumps along the way. For example, my nurses regularly sat me in a chair to get me up and out of my bed. Because my joints didn't work correctly, they had to strap me in. Unfortunately, one day they forgot the strapping part, and I ended up sliding down onto the floor. It was at the time I could still just barely talk, and I couldn't use the nurses' call button there lying on the floor. Lucky for me, I could manage to whisper "Help... Help..." Someone came by my open door and heard me. Poor Edna was horrified!

As for me, I was unharmed and thought the whole thing was hilarious.

The passing months had brought tremendous progress. Because of my time in the medically-induced coma, I had a condition known as drop foot, where all the degraded ligaments and tendons wouldn't allow me to lift the front of my feet. Because of that, I didn't think I would ever be able to walk. By month five, however, I could get out of bed and walk, which was nothing short of a miracle and due primarily to my physical therapist Vanessa and my occupational therapist Leslie.

A talk valve in my trach, which I got installed around two months after the fire, allowed me to speak to my Mom when she called every day from home in Tennessee. It was wonderful to have that connection with her. Seventy-eight then and long retired from her career at Austin Peay State University, Mom worked (as a volunteer) daily with my sister Debbie administrating the office of a local Civitan Club, and she would schedule monthly in-person visits to us in Massachusetts around my sister's own lifelong medical problems.

In fact, considering my sister, all I had to do to pull myself out of pity parties was to think about what Debbie had been through in her fifty-six years. She had been diagnosed with diabetes at the age of six with a prognosis that she wouldn't live over the age of thirty-five. She'd been through two kidney transplants, was legally blind, and had been hospitalized by countless infections.

Despite all that, she had a daughter, three grandchildren, and she worked at the Civitan every weekday with Mom. She was the true definition of a tough survivor.

By month six, I got some amazing news. "You're acting like a survivor, Diana," one of my surgeons told me. "Your progress has been amazing, and we think you're about ready to move to Spaulding rehab."

Finally, I felt like I was moving forward; it felt like I was getting closer to going home.

My Fight Song

This is my fight song
Take back my life song
Prove I'm alright song
My power's turned on
Starting right now I'll be strong
I'll play my fight song
And I don't really care if nobody else believes
'Cause I've still got a lot of fight left in me
*—**Fight Song** by Rachel Platten*

<u>Diana</u>

"Hi, Diana. Welcome to Spaulding. I'm Eugenia, and I'll be your head nurse during your stay."

I wasn't sure what to think of this woman at first. Between her thick accent, which made it difficult for me to understand her, and her serious demeanor, which reflected a no-nonsense attitude, I feared that she and I, with my sarcastic sense of humor, were a mismatched pair and wouldn't mesh well.

Then Eugenia took me to my room, which was located directly beside the nurse's station and had a window. "I saw in your file that you sometimes struggle with anxiety, so I thought being here, where you can see us and know we're here if you need us, would help." This incredibly thoughtful decision knocked my first impression on its head and was just the first of many indications that life at Spaulding would be different.

Arriving at Spaulding was like a breath of fresh air, in contrast to where I'd spent the last six months. Spaulding was light to Mass General's darkness. Perhaps that's just the nature of the different function of each. The hospital is for attempting then ensuring bare survival in the present, full of surgeries and near-dying on a daily basis; while rehab is for building on that survival to an active, productive future.

The nurses and therapists at Spaulding were upbeat and optimistic, communicating from day one their expectation that I would eventually walk out of their facility on my own, unlike a number of the burn staff at Mass General, who spent so many months trying to help Jerry come to terms with the 'fact' that I wouldn't survive.

At Spaulding, instead of a patient, they referred to me as a resident, and instead of medical staff, I had a team who had been training and studying my charts for months prior to my arrival. As the first patient to receive coordinated care between Dr. Goverman from

Mass General and the Spaulding staff, my care would become the standard practice for coordinated care from then on.

Despite all the positives, I was still in rough shape. I had absolutely no Activities of Daily Living (ADLs) skills. That is, I couldn't dress myself, shower by myself, or do a myriad of other basic daily activities. I had tubes coming out of every orifice in my body. Just getting me into a semi-standing position on the upraised walker they had modified for me took five nurses and therapists.

Because I had been bedridden for so long, all of my muscles had atrophied. My ankles were skewed, and the muscles in them had contracted and wanted to stay that way. My feet had not been burned from just above the ankles down, but there was scarring there because the surgeons had to use that skin for donor sites to graft on the third-degree burns that covered the rest of my body.

Both of my arms were grotesquely misshapen because, during my initial hypermetabolic state, Hypertrophic Ossification (HO) or overgrowth had occurred; additional bone formed on the outside and insides of my elbows, making it impossible for me to bend them.

I couldn't imagine what the therapists thought when they had their first conversations or sessions with me. I couldn't stand, I couldn't use my arms, and I couldn't even pick anything up with my hands.

Nonetheless, I had already beaten all the odds by making it to Spaulding. With this amazingly positive and well-trained team at my side, I got my first glimmer of hope that there might be a real life somewhere in my future.

Jerry

Something was wrong.

I knew it in my heart and soul.

When Diana moved to Spaulding Rehab, she was so excited. She called me the day she arrived, talking about her room and the nice paramedics who brought her to the hospital. She was full of hope and energy.

But when I arrived for my daily visit on her second day, I could tell immediately that something was very wrong. Diana was barely coherent.

"What's going on?" I asked the nurses. "Is she on meds?"

"Nothing out of the ordinary," they responded. That didn't make any sense. *If she's not drugged up, why is she so out of it?*

I looked at the urine bag, and it was almost completely empty. The anxious pit that had formed in my gut the second I entered the room tightened. "What does this mean? There's no urine here."

"She's not peeing. And she's got a fever too." Fever. Infection. The nervous pit exploded into full-blown panic.

"She needs to go back to Mass General," I insisted.

"Yes, she's scheduled to go on Monday. The doctor is gone for the weekend."

"No," I told them. "No, she is going right now if I have to carry her on my back."

Diana hadn't gotten many infections since her burn, but when she did have them, they were severe and needed to be treated aggressively and quickly. These new nurses didn't know her like I did. They didn't understand how unlike herself she was behaving. I had been told that she would be out of the woods when she made it to Spaulding, but in that moment, I was sure she was in immediate danger.

I was insistent, the annoying squeaky wheel who wouldn't let up. They tried to keep me calm, but I wouldn't back down.

She needed to go immediately. I knew my girl, they didn't, and it needed to be *right then*.

"She won't survive until Monday," I told them. "And I'm not going to watch my girl die! Call Dr. Goverman." The nurses tried to talk me out of it, but I persisted.

"She's got an infection, doc," I told him when I finally got him on the phone.

"She needs to come back now," he told the nurses. And then things started to happen.

He met me in the emergency room at Mass General, where I learned she was in renal failure. He sent her immediately up to the ICU and put her back on life support. They put her on dialysis and cleaned all her blood.

I visited her every day because I loved her, because I wanted to see her, and because I wanted her to know I cared about and believed in her, but I am sure she would have died had I chosen not to visit *that* day.

Later, we found out that Mass General and Spaulding weren't communicating, and the Spaulding doctors had added something to her medication cocktail that had shut down her kidneys.

Meanwhile, as I watched my angel fight for her life, I once again had people telling me things I didn't want to hear. One nurse suggested I not resuscitate her if she went into cardiac arrest.

"Why are you talking about a heart attack? Is she in danger of having one?" I asked her.

"No, but in case…"

"Then why did you bring that up?"

I was a mess.

Yes, Diana was in a coma again.

We had come so far, now only to seem to be going back to where we began.

I frantically called my friends and my pastor, preparing for the worst and praying for another miracle.

We weren't out of the woods; we were in the thick of them.

But I knew, I put my faith in the knowledge that Diana and I could conquer anything with the grace of God.

Diana

The initial hiccup in my transition from Mass General to Spaulding resulted in a near-death experience that put me back at Mass General for an entire month. Getting off of life support and recovering from the renal failure was rough, but at least I got to have chocolate cake when we celebrated my fifty-fifth birthday there.

Once I finally made it back to Spaulding, I settled into a comfortable groove with the care team I had met only briefly the last time around. Dr. Schneider, my Physiatrist/Rehab doctor and confidant, didn't just pop into my room for the obligatory daily visit. He would come in—usually having to clear the bandaging, tape, and scissors off of a chair in order to have a place to sit—and we would talk for at least fifteen minutes. We discussed my life before the burn, medical issues, weaning off pain medications, the weather, and anything else that struck our fancy.

My nurse, Rachel, was a breath of fresh air, too.

"Ooh nice pink undies," I teased her, as I caught sight of her underwear while she was leaning over the sink to wash her hands before changing my bandages.

Rachel promptly turned around and showed me the front of her panties, saying, "Aren't they pretty? They're striped." I laughed out loud at her response. Between her fun, quirky sense of humor and the music coming from my bedside CD player, I knew bandaging today would be fun, even if it was still painful.

"Let's see what we can do to get these things to stay on during therapy today, shall we?" she asked as she moved toward my bed with a tray full of antibacterial ointment, moisturizing ointment, abdominal pads, gauze pads, and Kurlix. She bopped along to the beat of the custom country music CD another nurse's husband—who was a DJ for a country music radio station—had made for me.

"I don't see why we even need to worry about it," I groused. "That silly nonsense Sammy makes me do in occupational therapy doesn't even do anything, and all

Jame cares about is taking her goniometer measurements so that she has something to report back to the doctors."

Rachel gave me a stern look. "Diana, you know that isn't true. Just because Sammy is smart enough to make your therapy not feel like therapy doesn't mean it isn't making a difference. Look at how much progress you've made! When you got here, you couldn't even pick anything up with your hands, and now you can feed yourself!"

I still felt grumbly, but I had to admit, she had a point. Before I could think up another argument, she pressed on.

"And as for Jame, do you know what all her measurements show? That you are improving! Since you've been working with her in physical therapy, your range of motion has gotten so much better."

Rachel's rebuttal pulled me up short. She was right. Despite the constant pain and severe limitations I endured during five hours a day of therapy, I had made big strides since arriving at Spaulding. My team was working hard for me, and I owed it to them to work just as hard for myself.

"Fine," I grudgingly agreed. "Bandage me up, and I'll do my best to make them all come loose during therapy." Rachel returned my impish smile with a grin of her own and got to work.

A few hours later, I could feel a smile form on my face as I heard Sammy come down the hall to take me to occupational therapy. She was singing that song by Sugarland, "Whoa-oh Woah-oh, Woah-oh…stuck like glue. Me and you, baby, we're stuck like glue."

It really was a great team!

Jerry

I could hear the arguing before I even got to the room. "I don't want to go to the gym today," Diana complained. She'd been working hard on her rehab for months now, but clearly, she was in a mood today.

As I rounded the corner and entered the room, I saw her sitting in bed wearing the bright red men's 3XL button-down shirt and matching fuzzy ankle socks. The combination might have seemed strange to an outsider, but Diana loved getting to choose her daily color scheme. Wearing real clothes made her feel more human. I'd gone shopping and bought her a rainbow's worth of options after noticing the other residents at Spaulding wore workout clothes in the gym. I wanted that for Diana, too, but with all her bandaging, she couldn't exactly wear sweats and T-shirts. The men's button-downs were a compromise that allowed her some control of her fashion choices while still accommodating the bulk of her bandaging.

"Honey, I know you're tired, but doing your physical therapy is important," Jess coaxed Diana.

Jess had taken over from Jame as Diana's physical therapist. Diana called her 'Little Mussolini' for all her tough firmness. While demanding and firm, she was also always ready with a smile. She and Diana had a good relationship, even on days like this one when Diana was cranky.

Diana wasn't having it. "I don't have to go," she argued. "Not if Jerry says I don't have to." Diana turned her pleading gaze on me, clearly expecting me to have her back against her physical therapist.

Of course, I had her back. I always had Diana's back, which is why I said, "I'll see you in the gym," before I turned and headed down hallway for the gym.

"Where do you think you're going?" Diana shouted after me as she hobbled along slowly with her walker. "Jerry, you get back here! I'm not going to the gym today. Jerry, come back!"

I grinned to myself as I continued on my way, waving to the staff I passed, all of whom called out, "Good afternoon, mayor," to Diana as she passed. Their nickname for her never failed to crack me up.

A few minutes later, we arrived at the gym. Diana was boiling mad, and I did my best to suppress my laughter as I turned to face her. "Since we're already here," I reasoned, "maybe you should go ahead and do your physical therapy."

If looks could kill, I would have been a pile of ash on the floor. Nonetheless, Diana eventually relented and got started on the workout Jess had laid out for the day.

The Woman in the Mirror

If it reads like depression
If it reads broken home
He's the One who holds your sorrow
He won't leave you here alone
—***God Is In This Story*** *by Big Daddy Weave and Katy Nichole*

<u>Diana</u>

The searing pain blocked everything else out.

Hermine, my wonderful nurse's aide, danced and sang, doing her very best to cheer me up. More times than not, her silly, playful performances would transform even the worst of mornings into a good one. She could sing out, "Hey Momma, Hey Momma, Hey Momma, Hey Momma," as she passed me in the hall, and a smile would bloom on my face. Today, though, nothing could take my mind off the pain. Tears streamed down my face as I struggled not to cry out, to beg and plead, and to do everything in my power to make it stop.

I had just returned to Spaulding from a stint at Mass General where I'd undergone my third round of debriding on my scalp. Because of a mechanical malfunction during a skin graft in one of my earlier surgeries, I had an open wound on the top of my head.

(The malfunction was the machine going too deep and taking the hair follicles—and hair will not grow back through grafted skin. The skin that was harvested was used for grafts on my wrist, forearm, and elbow, which are still growing the head hair—*ta-da!* These days, I have a full head of hair via a custom hairpiece blended into the hair on the back of my head—*LOL!*)

The debriding was just another attempt to scrape off the infection-ridden layers of tissue that were preventing the wound's healing in the hope that it would finally close.

My faith in the process was pretty well destroyed. The two previous attempts had failed, and after a short two-week period during which it looked like the third time might be the charm, things had taken a turn. Even if they could guarantee it would work, I wasn't sure it would be worth it.

Part of the post-procedure instructions was that my nurses had to remove the bandages for one hour every day in order to air the wound site. It only took about two minutes for the pain of the air colliding with the newly revived and exposed nerves to cause such a searing pain that I didn't think I would survive it. It felt like my head was on fire, but unlike the day of my accident, I could feel every second of the pain.

After only ten minutes, I broke. "Please, Hermine, please. Put the bandages back on. I can't take it anymore." My words must have been difficult to understand, garbled as they were by my sobbing, but Hermine knew what I was asking.

"Oh, Diana, I'm so sorry. I wish I could, but these are the doctor's orders. I know it hurts, but he thinks the airing will help the procedure to work this time so that you don't have to go back and do it again." Her logic was sound, and I knew it was her job to follow the doctor's orders, but that didn't change the fact that the pain was unbearable. My entire existence since the burn was one big haze of pain, and I liked to think I tolerated it pretty well, but this was unlike anything I had experienced. Nothing—not the pain of bandaging or recovery from my many surgeries—compared to the agony of having my scalp wound left uncovered.

"Please, Hermine. I have MRSA and VRE, [Methicillin-Resistant Staphylococcus Aureus and Vancomycin-Resistant Enterococci, two deadly infections], and we're in a hospital. Surely leaving open wounds exposed can't be safe and hygienic, can it?" I had no idea whether what I was saying made sense, but I would say anything, do anything, to get her to end my suffering. "Besides, I can't take it anymore. I just can't. Please, please re-wrap me."

Her face showed me how conflicted she was. A quick glance at the clock showed that only thirty minutes had elapsed since she had taken off the bandaging, but the sight of her weakening had me doubling down on my begging.

Finally, she relented. "Fine, I'll re-wrap it now, but don't tell the doctor. And re-wrapping early just means moving on to your shower sooner." Dread tightened my gut at her words, but not even my fear of showering could eclipse my relief at having my scalp wounds re-covered.

As soon as she had my scalp wrapped, Hermine began to unbandage the rest of my body to prepare for my shower. Once I was fully uncovered, she and another nurse's aide helped me up into a wheelchair so that she could wheel me down to one of the two showers on the floor. Fortunately, there was no line. It was always awkward when I had to sit there naked but for a blanket and wait half an hour or more for my turn in the showers.

As Hermine moved me into the shower, I felt the panic set in. Would today be the day that I drowned? Most people don't fear drowning in the shower, but that's because they don't have a trach. Having my trach in meant that any exposure to water was a risk. All it would take was an errant swipe of the shower head as Hermine was rinsing me off, and my lungs would fill with water.

Sensing my growing distress, Hermine reassured me. "Now Diana, you know I won't let anything happen to you. I know it makes you nervous on my days off when those other nurses' aides who aren't used to you have to do your showers, but you and me, we do this every day. And if today is the day that I accidentally drown you," she said, grinning to let me know she was teasing, "well, Steve is right down the hall. He's always talking about what strong lungs you have. I'm sure you could just cough the water right up, but even if you didn't, I'd be able to go grab him, and he'd get you straightened out, no problem."

The reminder that my respiratory therapist was readily available to help was encouraging. Even without the threat of being drowned in the shower, someone had to suction me regularly—a hazard of having a trach and spending so much time lying in bed. Every time my lungs filled with fluid, a sense of panic threatened to overtake me, but Steve made sure everyone knew how to help me out. Even therapy with him was fun, singing "Knock Three Times on the Ceiling" and goofing off instead of blowing into those dumb tubes and whatever other nonsense the other RTs made their patients do.

Calmed by the reminder that I had a fantastic team working not only to keep me alive but also to help me reclaim my independence, I relaxed and settled in for my shower.

Jerry

As I walked into the gym where Diana did physical therapy, the sight before my eyes shot through me like a sucker punch to the gut. My sweet, beautiful angel was sobbing uncontrollably.

"What happened?" I asked Jame, her physical therapist, even as I moved toward my girl.

Jame looked abashed. "I'm so sorry," she replied. "I forgot to check the mirror before I went to get her for therapy today. She saw her reflection."

The pain in my gut loosened some at the news. While it wasn't ideal, it also wasn't as bad as I'd feared. She hadn't injured herself. The emotional pain she was suffering—while significant—was both inevitable and something we could overcome. Her psychiatrist had ordered all mirrors to be covered and that she not be allowed to see herself, so this was the first time since the accident that she had seen her own reflection. I knew it would be a shock, but I also knew that this day would have to come, eventually. As I finally made it over to Diana, I did what I could to comfort her. I longed to take her into my arms, to hold her and remind her with my touch that she was still mine and I loved her, but her bandaging and injuries made that impossible. Determined to provide her with all the comfort I could, I used my words instead.

"Oh, baby, I'm so sorry. I know this is hard. Go ahead and cry, Diana. Cry as much as you need to. You deserve it. I'll be here when you're done if you want to talk. Just remember, I still love you."

Diana

"Just remember, I still love you," he had said. As I lay in bed that night, hours after Jerry had left, still sobbing uncontrollably, his words echoed through my head.

How could he say that to me?

I'd seen myself today for the first time since the accident. I'd seen what I'd become, and it was horrific. Gruesome. Disgusting. I look like Gollum from *Lord of the Rings*, a twisted, distorted version of humanity that no one could possibly love. Why was Jerry even still coming to visit me? Was it guilt? Was he worried people would judge him for leaving me in my condition? They wouldn't. Nobody would, not even me. Who could judge a man for not wanting to stay with such a horrific monster?

As another wave of despair washed over me, I heard someone entering my room. Turning to the door, I saw my night nurse, Amanda Darling.

"Oh sweetie," she murmured. "I heard what happened today. How are you?" Her forehead wrinkled as she seemed to register her own words. "Sorry, that was a silly question. Obviously, today was not a good day. What can I do to help?"

I sniffled through my non-stop flow of tears as her words rolled around in my head. What could she do to help? What could anyone do to help? I may not have been some supermodel bombshell before the accident, but I thought I was reasonably pretty. Now, I looked melted and disfigured. No one could fix that.

Suddenly, a thought struck me. Amanda couldn't change the way I looked, but there was one thing she could do to help. "Could I have a hug?" I asked through my tears.

Amanda had a superpower; she was the only one who could hug me without hurting me. It had been nine months since the fire, and I was deeply starved for touch. A touch. A feel. Closeness. An Amanda Darling hug was probably the only thing anyone could offer me at the moment that could help.

"Of course you can, Diana," Amanda replied as she moved closer and gave me one of her delicate hugs. I was far from better, but the comfort of that touch reached me on a soul-deep level.

Jerry continued to visit over the next few days, and I continued to cry. On the third day, his ability to provide silent comfort while I cried seemed to snap.

"Please, Diana," he begged. "Tell me what I can do to make this better, please. I hate to see you suffering like this."

I finally broke down and confessed my fears to him. "How can you love somebody like me?" I asked, desperate for reassurance that I was positive he could not provide.

He grabbed both my shoulders and looked me straight in the eyes. Tears started streaming down his face. It was the first time I had seen him cry since the accident, and the sight terrified me. Was this it? Was this the moment he admitted he couldn't love someone like me—that no one could?

"Because I love you," he said. "I didn't love you for the way you looked. What have you lost? A little skin? You haven't lost yourself. You're still you. My love for you isn't skin deep. I love Diana. You're still Diana, right? Or have you changed? Are you still Diana?"

I wiped some tears away. "I'm still Diana."

"Then, I still love you." He delivered the words in such a serious, solemn fashion that I couldn't doubt his sincerity. It took a while, but his words were the first step in healing that emotional wound. I might have only just seen myself, but Jerry had seen what I looked like every day of the past nine months. And all that time, every single day, he looked at me like he loved me.

Like I was beautiful.

Going Home

> *Being challenged in life is inevitable, being defeated is optional.*
> —Roger Crawford

Jerry

Before her discharge from Spaulding, Diana went on a series of outings in order to graduate from rehab. I still hadn't gotten over how upset Diana was at seeing her reflection for the first time, and I was terrified that this first public outing would result in rude stares or nasty comments that might set her back again.

One of our first outings was to the mall. As we made our way towards the escalator, I shot death glares at anyone whose gaze lingered a bit too long on Diana's scarred, bandaged form.

"Jerry," she scolded. "Quit giving everyone the stink eye and help me make sure I don't die on this escalator."

[*Aside from Diana: I was terrified of escalators <u>before</u> the burn. Call it severe escalator phobia. One misstep, and I pictured myself* *rolling down the escalator and being torn apart by the sharp edges at the bottom.*]

Diana didn't seem concerned about what other people thought of her or her appearance; instead, she focused on navigating the crowded mall with her walker.

"You'd think people would be considerate enough to give a cripple some space," she told me in her typical dry humor.

Diana's self-deprecating comment was delivered with such sincere disbelief that I couldn't help but snort out a laugh. "This is Boston, Diana. If you were expecting compassion and consideration, you're in the wrong place."

Her grumblings continued as she successfully stepped off the escalator.

Later, we stopped at a sushi restaurant for lunch. The place was packed, with barely enough room to navigate between tables, so Diana had to leave her walker at the door. I could tell she was nervous and unsteady, but she wound her way successfully through the space and down a short flight of stairs to our table. When our food arrived, we realized we'd forgotten her specially constructed fork and knife, but she still managed just fine. I was very proud of her. Through sheer tenacity, she crushed each new challenge set before her. There would be growing pains, and I would be there every step of the way if she needed me, but during those outings, I became hopeful about the future we would have together.

Diana

In order to show the staff at Spalding that I could survive outside the hospital and return home, Jerry and I stayed in a 'transitional living apartment.' The purpose of this exercise was to live together in a semi-controlled setting to prove to ourselves and my doctors that we could do it without many problems.

Jerry was confident in his ability to take care of me, but his first bandaging experience was difficult for both of us. We were completely by ourselves, just us and the bandages. I was getting frustrated with him because he was doing it differently than the nurses, not following their exact sequence of layering the bandages.

[*Aside from Jerry: I took her comments as a sign of her lack of confidence in me, which might be completely justifiable since I felt responsible for her being in this condition.*]

Our emotions were running high, filled with all the stress and anxiety of what we had gone through. We both felt this was a test to ensure he was ready to take care of me at home. He wanted to instill confidence in me, and I wanted to believe in him. By the end, we both had meltdowns and were in tears. That experience taught us it would have to be a joint effort going forward—forever, not just for an hour or two a day when Jerry visited me.

The week before my release was Easter Sunday, over 400 days since the burn. Mom, Jerry, and I walked into our small church together for the first time since that fateful day, and I felt the pressure mounting. This wasn't just a church service for me. It was also my last outing, my final exam before I graduated from Spaulding and finally returned home. Worshippers packed the church, and I felt the panic from the mall outing all over again. *What if someone bumped into me or knocked me over?* An injury might delay my release from Spaulding.

Glancing over at Jerry, I let his presence comfort me. I knew he would pick me up and carry me out of the church if I fell. He would rebandage me if the bandages came loose. And with his firm, supportive presence, I couldn't imagine anyone would come close enough to bump into me. He would be there for me.

"As we celebrate this Resurrection Sunday," the pastor began, "we have the honor of celebrating another of the Lord's miracles: Diana Tenney, brought back from the brink of death, is here with us today."

His words brought me back to the moment, and I looked at Jerry to see tears in his eyes. I knew he felt the truth of the pastor's words just as strongly as I did. My recovery was a miracle, one that I thanked God for every day.

Despite how well things were going, the prospect of going home the following week still made me nervous. What if something happened? I would no longer have my team of medical professionals just a few steps away, able to handle the more severe needs that Jerry couldn't. Still, Jerry's confidence in his ability to take care of me and God's faithfulness through our journey so far provided reassurance in the face of my worries.

After the church services ended, we headed to a friend's house for Easter dinner. My hypermetabolic state had dropped my weight from one hundred thirty-five to one hundred pounds, leaving me constantly hungry. Everyone at the dinner table was shocked—and impressed—when I put away three full plates of ham, dressing, and mashed potatoes. It was the first home-cooked meal I'd enjoyed in over a year, and I relished enjoying it so much with friends.

Jerry

There was a lot to do to get ready for Diana's return. I installed an AC unit to keep her from overheating, then rearranged the closets and storage space to make room for all of her clothes to be moved to the first floor so she wouldn't have to navigate the stairs.

[*Aside from Diana: Of course, we would wind up moving everything back upstairs, because, if anything, stairs were therapy. Plus, upstairs had been, and was, my space, and I was more than ready to reoccupy it.*]

An elevated toilet seat, rails in the shower and leading up the front steps, and a new Tempur-Pedic mattress were just a few of the upgrades I made to ensure our home was comfortable and accessible for her.

Insurance didn't cover any of those things, but our amazing support group of friends helped me do some fundraisers, which more than covered the costs. There was even money left over, which I put into a trust to help cover Diana's ongoing medical expenses.

After all that, I had just one thing to do. The roof tiles on our house needed to be replaced. The contractor came out, and while we were standing outside, discussing colors and options, I looked up and noticed that our neighbor's house was also badly in need of a new roof. As always, Corey was outside tending to his yard, so I hollered for him to come over.

"Hey, Jerry. What's up? You getting a new roof?" he asked.

"Yep, sure am, and so are you. Pick your tile color."

"Ah, no, that'd be nice, but I can't afford that."

I fixed him with a stern gaze before replying, "You don't have to be able to afford it. I'm paying."

Shock colored his features before what looked like wounded pride mixed in. "Jerry, you're a good guy, but I don't need your charity," he said stiffly.

"Of course, you don't need my charity, Corey, and this ain't charity. You saved Diana's life. She's coming home soon, and all because you acted. My girl was on fire. She would have burned to death if not for you." The sudden swell of emotion caught in my throat as memories of that horrible day assailed me. "A new roof for your house is a sorry excuse for a thank you for saving the life of the woman I love, but it's the best I can do."

With a somber nod, Corey walked over to the contractor to pick the roof tiles he wanted.

Diana

April 29, 2011, "D Day"—discharge day—had finally arrived. Jerry ordered pizzas for all the Spaulding staff, and I hosted a farewell party. It felt like my first step in returning to normal life. Hosting get-togethers had always brought me joy. I loved feeding the staff and showing each one of them my appreciation for all their hard work in caring for me and assisting in my recovery over the long months. While I knew God was ultimately responsible for the miracle of my healing, I was under no illusions about the amount of work my surgeons at Mass General and the team at Spaulding had put into getting me to where I was.

We had to leave before the night shift got there, but Jerry placed an order to have pizzas delivered for them as well, and the day shift promised to pass along my thanks and goodbyes as we made our tearful farewells. Although it was against the rules, my therapists and nurses had gotten together and given me a gardening bag complete with tools as a goodbye gift. Finally, I could fulfill my goal of walking out the door with only my two feet supporting me.

The car ride home was not fun because sitting in a car was incredibly uncomfortable thanks to all my scar tissue and the open wounds on the tops of my thighs and my backside. The emotional mess in my head compounded the physical pain.

As we rolled into New Bedford, I tried to enjoy seeing familiar sites and landmarks until it appeared Jerry was not going to our home.

"Just one stop," he said. We arrived at a church where an AA meeting was going on in the basement. "We need to go in and say thank you for all their prayers." I carefully maneuvered the stairs and entered the room, stopping the meeting mid-progress. They gave me a round of applause, nearly moving me to tears with their support.

The future was scary. While it was true that Jerry had gotten much better at bandaging, I was still a basket case as we left the hospital. Knowing I could no longer press a button to make healthcare professionals appear terrified me. It was still hard for me to lie down because of my abdominal burns. I had difficulty getting out of bed because I couldn't even sit up on my own, and somebody had to pull me up or roll me over; I was in constant danger of rolling off the bed. In the hospital, I had felt wrapped up in this little cocoon of care, and I wouldn't have that when we got home.

Still, I knew that if Jerry and I were to return to anything resembling normalcy, we had to make this leap.

It would just be Jerry and me against the world.

The New Normal

Maybe it's time to find a New Normal.
—*Trish Doller*

Diana

Waking up at home that first day was strange, and then it was strange that it was strange. I was in my house, the home I had shared with Jerry for eight years, and yet I'd been gone for so long that it felt like getting used to a new environment.

Still, I wasn't going to waste the newfound freedom that came with being out of the hospital.

My very first priority of the day was to head into the kitchen and make a pot of coffee. The contractures in my arms limited my mobility, so I had to use two hands to lift and pour the pot, but after a bit of effort, I made coffee.

A sort of girlish giddiness took hold of me as the rich, warm aroma filled the kitchen. At Spaulding, I'd only been allowed two cups a day. Now that I was home, I intended to drink that pot dry, down to the last drop.

Once I had finished, I decided to try to make some breakfast. I opened the cabinets, rummaging around for things, but quickly realized I couldn't reach any higher than the bottom shelf of the upper cabinets, thanks once again to my contractures. As I rummaged around in frustration trying to figure out how to accomplish my goal, Jerry entered the room.

"Here Diana, just let me do that," Jerry suggested sternly as he walked up behind me and took over.

Frustration and discouragement welled up inside me. I knew it wasn't in Jerry's nature to watch me struggle with something, but I also knew what a burden I was to him. Our relationship was so unbalanced, with him doing all the giving and me doing all the taking, and his refusal to let me try to shoulder some of the burdens by doing something as simple as making breakfast frustrated me.

There at that moment, some of my anger and resentment at my condition bubbled up and over onto him as I became angry. *Why couldn't he just let me try? Why couldn't he just let me do it myself?* If he didn't let me figure out how to do things on my own, I felt, I would never stop being a burden. *How long was he going to put up with that sort of thing here at home*, I thought, *before he got fed up and left me?*

Insecurity began to overwhelm me as I watched him move confidently around the kitchen. Jerry was everything: strong, handsome, loyal, and a good earner. It wouldn't be difficult for him to find someone else. And while I had come to terms with my scars and appearance, I still didn't see how he could stay with someone like me. That insecurity rolled around and wrapped me up tight until I was lashing out.

"I could have done that if you'd just been patient," I snapped.

Lucky for me, my mother was with us then, and "Diana, you know Jerry's just trying to help," she said quietly, soothing, as she entered the room. Her presence brought with it another wave of guilt. My sister relied heavily on my mother, and I knew how worried my mother was at being away from her. I felt so selfish for having her here, for needing her help as I transitioned back home. What was Deb back in Tennessee supposed to do while I was here taking up all of Mom's time and attention?

Feeling overwhelmed by the whole situation, I headed upstairs to get dressed.

Later that day, when the occupational therapist arrived, I convinced her to help me rearrange the cabinets so that all the things I needed to access regularly were within my reach. It wasn't much, but it was a small step towards giving me the sense of independence I knew I'd need in order to feel like I was a good partner to Jerry, or at least as good a partner as someone in my condition could be.

Jerry

"Unfortunately," said the uncomfortable-looking financial counselor from SHINE [Serving the Health Insurance Needs of Everyone, a National Organization], "Diana isn't eligible for Medicaid. She worked and paid in for a lot of years, which has made her Social Security Disability Insurance payment too high to qualify."

Despite his obvious desire to help, the unfairness of her situation landed like a punch to the gut as we sat across the desk while he continued sifting through our mountain of paperwork. Diana was one of *those* people—the people who fall through the cracks. She had worked since the age of sixteen and was fortunate enough to make more than most without a college degree, but now, in her time of need, she was being penalized for it.

"Okay, so what do we do?" I asked. "The private insurance is too expensive for her to afford on her SSDI payment. Without supplemental insurance, we won't be able to afford the reconstructive surgery copays."

"There is a program called 'working disabled' for which she would be eligible."

Diana and I exchanged a look. She was going to be in and out of the hospital for surgeries a lot over the next couple of years, and the recovery often left her severely fatigued.

"If Diana accepts a job and ends up having to quit because she can't keep up with it," I tried to reason. "She'll lose the income from her job, her SSDI payment, and won't be able to reapply for disability because she hasn't sustained a new injury since she got off it. Plus, who is going to hire her with her mobility issues, scarring, and missing work every other month because of surgeries and recovery?"

The crushing weight of defeat settled on my shoulders. Diana's discharge was supposed to mark the end of the difficult road we'd been on for so long, and in many ways, it did. In others ways, however, the struggle was only beginning. Trying to navigate the healthcare system for Diana was a bureaucratic nightmare. It had been a struggle from the very beginning, ever since she was first burned in March 2010. But the real problems began in September, when we started trying to fill out her Medicaid/Mass Health insurance paperwork.

I had assumed that the Massachusetts health representative who had been with us throughout

Diana's hospital stay would help us, but I was wrong. We couldn't even apply for Medicaid until after she was fully discharged, at which point she was no longer the hospital's problem, so we were left to navigate the convoluted system on our own.

The SHINE counselor wasn't our first stop. I'd already had to hire a lawyer just to help us get through all the red tape. *How do people without a partner or family member to help them deal with all this?* I wondered. *How do they pay their bills?*

"Jerry, you're self-employed, right?" The counselor's question tore me out of my frustrated thoughts and brought me back to the moment.

"Yes, I own my own business. Though, yeah, self-employed sounds right, as I don't have any employees."

"How would you like to have one?" he suggested, and my eyebrows wrinkled in confusion. *Is this guy trying to get me to hire her?*

"If you hire Diana," he advised us, "and keep her pay within the limits allowed by disability, then she could qualify for Medicaid as 'working disabled'."

"Oh, that makes sense. I mean, it wouldn't bring any additional income into the household, but if it would help her qualify for all the benefits she needs, then I'm for it."

"Great!" The counselor gave us a big smile. "So, the only thing is that you can only pay Diana $30 a month, and no more than $700 over the course of three years, or she'll lose her disability benefits."

"$30 a month?" I was disgusted. How were people ever supposed to get off disability if they could only earn $30 a month while they recovered?

"I know it's frustrating. Not to rub salt in the wound, but be sure to keep in contact with me. The rules and regulations are constantly changing. You don't want to be caught up by regulatory changes you didn't know about."

It seemed an awful lot like the system was designed to keep people in it, rather than helping them get out and become self-sufficient. But there was no way for Diana to support herself financially without losing all her benefits. They were destroying any incentive to work by making sure there was no safety net if someone tried to rejoin the workforce and things didn't work out.

The counselor was right, it was a way to make it work, just the way the system demanded. We had and have nothing but thanks for that SHINE counselor's precious bit of advice.

And we put it to work. And her…. for $30 a month.
[*Aside from Diana: And I earned every bit of it!*]

Diana

I typed out the final few words in my email.

After learning that typing was wonderful therapy for my fingers, I made it my mission to send emails thanking everyone who had been involved in the early stages of my care, back before I could interact with them directly. I sent messages to the firefighters, EMTs, the doctor at St. Luke's, the respiratory therapist at St. Luke's who intubated me, my med flight people—everyone.

Fortunately for my therapy efforts, the list was literally never-ending. There were friends, church members, high school classmates, Facebook friends, and more. The more I thought, the more people I realized had a hand in my recovery.

Finally finished, I clicked send on the email and minimized the window before heading downstairs. The ladies from my unsanctioned AA group, A Way of Life (AWOL), were coming over later, and I needed to go to the store to get everything to make the snacks.

"How about trying Whole Foods today?" Dee, my PCA, asked as I climbed into the car.

"Absolutely not," I replied, recoiling in disgust.

"Wow, okay, that was a strong reaction. Wanna tell me what that was about?"

"Bad experience. I had to go there to shop for groceries as a part of my transitional phase before I left

Spaulding, and the people were so unbelievably rude to me. I won't ever go back there."

"Okay," Dee asked, "where to?"

Once we pulled into the parking lot at the Stop and Shop grocery store, my excitement began to build. Hosting had always been one of my favorite activities, and I loved the opportunity to have a bunch of friends over and feed them. Despite my extremely high metabolism, I tried to keep my diet clean and nutritious, with a heavy emphasis on protein. I always served things like charcuterie boards and fruit and veggie trays, but with my own spin on things that made it all original and delicious. I was eager to gather my groceries so that I could get home, get everything prepped, and neatly displayed on my serving trays.

AWOL nights were always a blast, and I knew this one would be no different.

Jerry

Working from home was a huge blessing. It meant I was around to help Diana with all the little things she needed throughout the day, and was, without a doubt, one of the biggest perks of my job. Unfortunately, the downside that came with it was having to go on frequent sales calls, which meant I was sometimes hours away from her. This was a tremendous source of anxiety for me as we transitioned to having her back home. I didn't love having to travel so far away from her while she was in the hospital, but at least I knew she had people to take care of her. With her home now, I could never quite shake the worry that any given trip would be the one during which she needed me, and I wouldn't be there.

As I hit the road for yet another day of sales calls and presentations, worries about our finances crept into my mind. Going from a two-income household to just one was tough enough, but with Diana's medical expenses piling up, the strain was impossible to ignore.

Whenever those thoughts crept in, I brought myself back to the present. Getting too caught up in what might happen tomorrow led down a dark road I'd long since committed not to revisit. I'd always been a good earner, and God had always provided. I knew I just had to continue to trust in Him.

"How's your wife doing?" the distributor I was visiting asked. My clients always asked about her. They'd watched me go through the whole agonizing process, and their concern always warmed me.

"She's doing well," I replied with a smile. I didn't bother correcting people anymore about the fact that we weren't actually married.

"Oh yeah? How's having her back home? She's all

recovered now, right?"

"Not quite, no. She still has a long way to go, but we found her a great team. She has nurses, PCAs, an occupational therapist, and a physical therapist who all come to the house and help her. It's a lot of work, but she's a tough cookie."

Finding people who had experience with burn patients hadn't been easy, but I knew how working with people who lacked the experience stressed Diana. And it's not like her fears were irrational. She knew plenty of burn patients whose skin had torn from working with a physical therapist or other medical professionals who didn't understand the differences and limitations of grafted skin.

As I drove home after the meeting, my client's words drifted through my mind. *She's all recovered now, right?* Worries about the future came creeping in. Would Diana ever be "all recovered"? She'd already made it so much further than anyone expected, but would there be things that never got better? Things she could never do again? How would it affect her? Us?

With a shake of my head, I firmly cut off the spiral. I knew I needed to stay grounded in the present. With everything that had happened, I realized it was the simple things that mattered most. I didn't need to worry about tomorrow. If I took care of today, tomorrow would take care of itself. After all, none of us were guaranteed another day. And even though tomorrow would bring its own set of challenges, I knew I had the strength to face them when the time came. For the moment, I would focus on the present and keep on driving.

Diana

"Diana, are you out here?" called Dee, my friend-turned-PCA (personal care assistant).

"Yeah, we're pulling weeds," I replied.

The "we" was me and my occupational therapist (OT), who had learned quickly upon meeting me that I had no patience for structured therapy. I wanted to spend my time getting good at doing practical, useful things. Fortunately, she had graciously accommodated that, and so here we were, pulling weeds in the backyard for my therapy time.

"Well, is your session about finished? We need to get you showered," Dee replied. "Your nurse will be here to bandage you soon."

My OT nodded her acknowledgment that the hour was indeed up, so she helped me stand, and I headed inside.

An hour and a half later, I was showered and sitting around in a bathrobe, waiting not-so-patiently for the nurse—who was long overdue—to come to bandage me. The ringing of the bell alerted me to her arrival.

"About time," I grumbled as I answered the door. I knew I was being surly, but I liked to keep to a schedule and did not like waiting around in my bathrobe for her to arrive.

"Now, look here, missy," Sue, my home healthcare nurse, retorted. "You are not my only patient. The elderly gentleman I went to see before you had a rough time, and it took me longer than planned to get him sorted. I don't leave you before you're all taken care of just so that I can keep to a schedule, and I don't leave my other patients while they still need me either. Sometimes, that might mean that you have to wait a bit, but just be thankful for Jerry and Dee and the fact that I never find you in a state like I did that other man."

Thoroughly chastised, I sat quietly while she bandaged me. I did sometimes feel like I must be the worst-off person she visited. It was strange how I could be thankful to God each morning I woke and could walk to the kitchen and make myself a pot of coffee, and yet I still allowed my focus to narrow so far that I couldn't see anything beyond my own comfort and schedule.

Once she finished, Sue said, "I've been thinking about what you said about your thigh bandages falling down all the time. I thought we might try something different." With a sly grin, she pulled out some ribbons and netting to make a set of garters. A peel of laughter burst from me at the sight.

"Well, I'm certainly up for trying them. Dee is taking me to chair yoga after this, so we'll see if they're up to the challenge."

Here We Go Again

> *I won't be silenced*
> *You can't keep me quiet*
> *Won't tremble when you try it*
> *All I know is I won't go speechless*
> *—**Speechless** by Naomi Scott*

Diana

While receiving skin grafts was an amazing blessing that allowed me to survive, it also came with its challenges. The skin was so delicate that it couldn't handle sun exposure, which broke the heart of my inner sun goddess. One day, I actually burned a hole in a graft just by sitting outside on an unshaded picnic bench, while talking to my AA sponsor.

Not only was sun exposure a no-go, but the skin was incredibly tight and had no give to it. I always ate well thanks to horror stories I'd heard of other burn patients. We all experience a period during recovery where we can eat as much as we want without consequences, but eventually, our metabolism levels out, and then our grafted skin can't accommodate the weight gain that results. Stories of people's skin actually bursting were horrifying enough to make sure that I kept my diet centered on proteins, veggies, and supplements.

Not only did the tight skin make weight gain dangerous, but it also caused circulation and movement restrictions. This perpetual tightness necessitated an almost never-ending series of surgeries to release contractures caused by the tight grafts.

As I recovered from the initial shock and transition of finally returning home, I noticed that my body seemed to have a sort of prescience in how it could predict how long it would be until my next surgery. In the beginning, I would go back for reconstructive surgeries every forty-five days or so. My body rebounded from the side effects of anesthesia and the pain medication detox pretty quickly. After six months of that, I would only go back every three months for the surgeries, and the recovery took longer. When I started having the surgeries six months apart, it would take exactly six months for me to get my energy back and feel fully recovered, almost as if my body knew how long it had to recover and intended to use every available moment.

Between the risks of damaging my grafts, the constant state of recovery from the surgeries, and my tendency to injure myself without even realizing it due to nerve damage and losses of sensation to various areas of my body, doing inspections of my body became a daily part of my ritual.

Jerry and I grew accustomed to the chaos though, and eventually, not much phased us. If a staple got twisted up in my scar tissue, Jerry would pull it out with some pliers. If I discovered a surprise gash on my leg from having walked into a table or something, I would clean and bandage it.

We became so used to handling things on our own that we may have grown overconfident and failed to seek professional help when we really needed it.

When I got home after a massive thigh surgery, I subconsciously knew something was different. I shivered uncontrollably, unable to get warm. Still certain I could handle it on my own, I went to a sound meditation and took some immune supplements, hoping it would help with my recovery, but the shivering just got worse and worse every day. Then I got nausea and diarrhea at the same time. Yep, something was wrong.

"Maybe I shouldn't go," Jerry said, looking regretfully at the football tickets he had received from our friend Lynn. Guilt shot through me. Ever since the fire, I was always such a pain in the ass to Jerry. He'd restricted his entire life to accommodate my care, and now he couldn't even go enjoy a football game because

I wasn't recovering well from my latest surgery.

"Of course you should go," I argued. "So I don't feel great. So what? What are you going to do if you're here? Watch me be miserable? That's just silly. At least one of us should be able to enjoy ourselves. Go, have a good time."

He still looked reluctant, but I put on my best "I'm fine" face and shoved him out the door. I still felt horrible, but I wasn't lying about him not being able to do anything about it. Either I'd get over it, or I'd still be sick after the game, and him being with me wouldn't impact that at all.

Once I was alone, I took off the bandages and checked the wounds. They were a disgusting, putrid green, which I knew meant pseudomonas (a fungal infection that will kill you if you don't get it treated). I took photos and sent them to my surgeon, who told me to come in the next day for silver soaks.

When I arrived at the hospital, I expected to see my surgeons and doctors, but a group of fellows came to see me instead. Fellows, as in interns, which are young MDs fresh out of med school. Fresh and all very confident—they did actually graduate med school, didn't they? And all just as very much inexperienced.

But it goes to the fact of receiving treatment at a teaching, public hospital; one does not get to choose her providers, to pick and choose her doctors. In my case, all my experienced burn doctor teams were already always over-committed and over-worked, so, with something as everyday as a regimen treatment of silver soaks, it wasn't unusual to have the assignment sent to fellows/interns.

"I'm sorry, but we were assigned to you. Let me get you started on an IV, and your surgeon will be in to see you when he can."

Doing my best not to let my irritation show, I calmly explained, "My records clearly state that I have no veins and that I need a central line for IVs."

"Oh, don't you worry," one of the fellows said. "I'm great at hitting tricky veins. I'll be able to get your IV placed, no problem." His insane overconfidence and blatant refusal to listen to me or my chart were the first signs that this would not go well.

"We've tried this before," I told him. "You're going to see what looks like a vein, but it will be scar tissue. It's not going to work." He remained resolute, absolutely certain he'd be able to place an IV. Exhausted and frustrated, I finally agreed to let him try. After several failed attempts, another fellow tried. They played pincushion with me for a couple of hours before an anesthesiologist finally figured out that they couldn't find a vein to use.

By the time they put in a central femoral stick and started pumping Vancomycin, I was beyond frustrated.

The fellows announced they also wanted to try out an antibiotic called Cefepime, which I was unfamiliar with. I had no idea what they hoped this drug would achieve considering I'd come in for silver soaks, but by then I was beyond caring. Someone had finally placed the central line—who cared what they put in it?

After about an hour, I felt weak, feverish, and nauseated, and the longer they pumped the new drug, the worse I felt. It wasn't long before my temperature hit 106 degrees Fahrenheit, I swelled up like a Macy's Day balloon, and my skin turned brown, yellow, purple, and an assortment of other colors. Next, a rash appeared and quickly consumed my entire body, but my doctors still only sent their fellows, refusing to come up themselves.

"Ma'am," a nervous-looking intern said as he walked into the room. "We're not sure what is causing all this, but your condition is extremely severe. At this point, we're worried you may die of either a heart attack or renal failure."

While many people in my position might have been shocked or scared, I was pissed. This was far from my first time at death's door, but this time, they had caused it. I came in for silver soaks and suddenly had an intern telling me I was about to die.

[Aside from Jerry: By now, I trusted Diana's ability to advocate for herself. I couldn't read her mind right then, but I'm sure it was

along the lines of "This is déjà vu all over again".]

"You need to stop the Cefepime. I haven't felt right since you started it," I informed him. "When will the renal doctor and cardiologist be here?"

"Oh, we haven't called them. It's not the Cefepime, but we'll figure out what the problem is. Don't worry — we have this under control," the intern assured.

I stared slack-jawed at him, completely baffled by his words. *Under control?* Their so-called diagnoses and treatments were almost certainly what had caused my condition in the first place, and they were still refusing to stop the Cefepime, but they had things *under control*?

A few hours later, they broke, and the renal doctor finally came in to visit.

"Well," he began, "I don't know what's wrong with you, but it's not your kidneys. They may be the only part of you that is doing just fine."

Beyond fed up with the lack of answers and attention from the doctors, I threw off the covers and climbed out of bed.

"What are you doing?" an alarmed-looking nurse demanded.

"Going for a walk," I replied as calmly as possible. She looked like she might have a heart attack herself at my announcement, but I was beyond caring. As soon as I made it out the door, I headed for the gift shop. I still couldn't get warm, and the nurses had insisted they couldn't adjust the thermostat in my room, so I got myself a hoodie instead, and afterward I grabbed a Gatorade at Coffee Central. This became my daily routine over the next few days—argue with nurses, get ignored by doctors, go for a walk, and grab a Gatorade.

A few days in, my heart rate surged. The fellows, who'd already been worried about me having a heart attack, became even more alarmed. Fortunately, it turned out that the spikes in heart rate were being caused by all the Gatorade I was drinking and the bananas I'd been eating. As soon as I laid off those, my heart rate went back to normal. Unfortunately, that meant I was subjected to canned fruit, since bananas were the only fresh option the hospital had on offer.

Over the next week, my condition continued to deteriorate. The arrogant group of fellows/interns finally consulted a dermatologist, who diagnosed me with Henoch-Schoenlein Purpura (HSP), which usually presents in male patients under the age of nine.

Of course, only I could get a little boy's disease as a 55-year-old woman.

When Dr. Goverman came by for rounds later that day, I told him, "I don't know what HSP is, but what I do know is that my problems are being caused by the Cefepime, which these idiots refuse to take me off of." Dr. Goverman agreed to take me off the Cefepime, and I started improving almost immediately.

Unfortunately, the interns—for reasons I will never understand—put me back on it the next day.

Everyone continued to tell me I would not make it. Between the negativity and the grossly incompetent care I was receiving, I finally said, "If I'm not going to make it, I'm going to go home to die." By that time, I had developed solid blisters from my knees down to the bottom of my feet. Basically, I was burning from the inside out.

I demanded the Chief doctor for burns come to talk to me right away. They told me he was in surgery, so I began screaming at the nurses and fellows, and he showed up fifteen minutes later.

Looking him dead in the eye, I said, "I just want to know how it is that I came to the hospital for silver soaks, and I end up like this? When I came, I was not in this swollen state with all these pretty colors and a total body rash."

"I don't know," he said.

"Okay," I told him. "Here's what we're going to do. I haven't felt right since you started putting Cefepime in me. You're going to take me off of that. You can leave the Vancomycin in. You're going to give me Prednisone to reduce the swelling because I always do really well with that. And then, you're going to discharge me. I'm going home, and you can give me antibiotics if you want for when I get home."

He looked at me, then said, "Okay, I guess you know what you want, but you can't discharge today."

My plan was implemented, and the Prednisone immediately made my swelling go down. After ten days in the hospital, I was finally able to go home. By that point, I was seriously depressed from the questionable medical care and no one listening to me.

For the second time, I agreed to see a psychiatrist. With his encouragement, I wrote a letter to my care team a few months after my discharge, but nothing came of it. When I went in for my follow-up, a nurse practitioner met me instead of a doctor, and I lost it. Apparently fearful of being on the receiving end of my wrath once again, he asked if I wanted to speak with Dr. Goverman, and I said yes. That helped, but neither he nor anyone else had an explanation for what happened to me.

Resentment over this event consumed me for a long time, and I was very depressed about it. After a couple of weeks, I used a pair of oversized sneakers and got back into Zumba classes, which helped with my depression over the incident.

Things seemed to get better until I realized I was drooling from my neck when I ate. Another clinic trip only resulted in more confusion, until finally, they realized that all the swelling brought on by my adverse reaction to the Cefepime had caused a fistula in my submandibular salivary glands. The tiny hole broke apart my grafting enough to cause me to drool from my neck. It took two years of grossing out my friends and having to use stacks of napkins at every meal just to keep my neck dry before they finally decided they needed to remove the submandibular salivary gland in order to get it to stop.

That single, horrible incident had a years-long impact on my body, as well as my relationship with my doctors and my trust in the healthcare system.

Advocacy and Community

Sometimes I believe
That I can do anything
Yet other times I think
I've got nothing good to bring
But you look at my heart and you tell me
That I've got all you seek
—***Free to Be Me*** *by Francesca Battistelli*

Diana

"Even if she survives, she'll be a burden to you—a burden to society."

That's what the doctor, the one who suggested to Jerry all those months ago that perhaps he should let me die while I was in my coma.

As I moved from the "recovering" phase to the "this is my new normal" phase of life, my focus shifted from relearning basic skills to proving that doctor wrong. I was determined to do something, to make a difference, and not to spend the rest of my life sitting on my butt, burdening Jerry and society.

My drive to do something productive with my life, coupled with the struggles I'd faced during my recovery, led me to peer support and advocacy. Jerry has always maintained that the biggest factor determining who in the burn unit survived and who didn't was whether they had a loved one there advocating for them. It became a passion point for me to act as a patient advocate for those in the burn unit who had no one else. I got certified in a program from an international organization for burn survivors and started working with our local Burn Survivors of New England, where I ended up serving on the Board and became President, then later President and Treasurer, and finally President, Secretary, and Treasurer.

All these interactions led me to notice patterns in the people around me. I did a deep dive into the research on burn patients, hoping to facilitate my own recovery and help the people for whom I advocated. What I learned was astounding. There was not much out there, and what little burn research had been done disappeared into academic bookshelves, never to be used by doctors or accessed by patients and their advocates.

For example, six years after my burn, my vitamin D was so low that it sent me into hypoparathyroidism.

After digging around, I found some "bookshelf research" showing that burn survivors will have lifelong vitamin D deficiency, magnesium deficiency, and permanent bone loss. My surgeons, for all their expertise in handling my reconstructive surgeries, had communicated no information about these sorts of lifelong impacts. No one had ever prescribed me supplements to offset the impact of the burn on my body. Had I not done the research myself, I would still be in the dark.

All of my research and advocacy came together when I began working with Boston Harvard Burn Injury Model Systems, or BH-BIMS. I am so proud of the work we are doing there. With our focus on Patient Reported Outcome Measures, we were able to improve care and outcomes for burn patients all over America.

With the help of BH-BIMS staff, I was the first non-medical burn survivor to become a course director at the American Burn Association (ABA) Annual conference in 2019. We introduced the idea of burns as a chronic condition, and that is a work-in-progress. I have been "published" in medical journals as a co-author, mistakenly once noted as Dr. Tenney, (ha!).

I was on the ground-floor level and also the first enrollee of the Life Impact Burn Recovery Evaluation (LIBRE), which is a measuring tool for burn survivor recovery. My name was on a placard with the Harvard logo during a 3-day seminar Rwandan burn delegation.

I continue to be in on the ground floor and to work on projects that will probably not come to full fruition and use even in lifetime, but it's a start, and maybe it will make it better for burn survivors to come.

At a Christmas party for New England burn survivors, a woman named Kate approached me. She was a highly skilled massage therapist who wanted to work with burn patients and believed that careful application of massage therapy could help them regain some of the circulation and mobility they had lost to their injuries.

Because there wasn't really any research available on the subject, Kate needed a test patient. With my extensive scarring, she felt I would be the perfect guinea pig to figure out which techniques and approaches would be most effective in working with burn patients.

I was hesitant—I know, who passes on free massages? But burned skin is delicate and easily torn. In the end, I agreed to let her try her methods on me.

The results were astounding. The first time I went to her, she put her hands on my temples and said, "God, Diana, what is wrong emotionally?"

I gave her my standard answer. "Oh, I'm fine. Nothing's wrong."

She continued with some cranial massage. But when I got home, I just let go and cried. Then, I noticed that the next day was my burn accident anniversary. I hadn't even noticed, but clearly, I must have remembered subconsciously, and Kate could sense that tension and help release it using massage.

After a lot of experimentation, she came up with a system of light myofascial massage, which helped with blood flow, a lot of lymphatic work, and craniosacral massage. It made such an enormous difference in my healing that I ended up teaming up with her to form The Massage and Burn Scar Therapy Foundation, a non-profit offering massage to burn patients.

While insurance, hospitals, and rehab centers are still not willing to pay for burn scar massage, the many patients who have benefitted will attest to the tremendously positive mental and physical impact it has had on their healing.

Jerry

Step by step, Diana found her way and became more independent. Her recovery brought me so much joy, and also freed up a lot of my time. Finding myself at loose ends and wanting to give back to my community, I began spending a few days a week working in a detox center, which I found very rewarding. It felt like a calling, so I went back to school online during COVID to acquire a certificate in counseling. From my own recovery journey with alcohol to helping Diana through her burn recovery, I have seen the beauty of finding someone who is lost in darkness and how life changing it can be when someone reaches out to help.

God willing, I will continue to be a helping hand to those around me who are suffering.

Diana

I was in a movie.

Somebody from the burn network called me and suggested that I audition for a role in the indie film, *Chained for Life*, because they were looking for a burn survivor. I had already done some burn survivor videos for the Burn Model System's website, so I applied for shits and giggles, never thinking I really had a chance.

They sent the script, and Jerry and I shot the audition video on our personal camera with the help of a friend. I just read it normally—I didn't even practice. They also asked for a short "about me" video interview, which I recorded and sent in.

Almost immediately, they called to offer me the

part. We discussed the pay—they paid for all my travel and hotel expenses, plus twenty-five dollars an hour—and I signed on for the movie.

Chained for Life was a dark comedy set in the thirties that focused on how Hollywood treats people with disabilities and physical differences. Today, they have inclusivity quotas, and more types of bodies and people with disabilities are portrayed in television and movies, but anyone who is more than ten years old knows it hasn't always been that way. The writer/director was Aaron Shimberg, a man with a cleft palate who understood what it was like to be treated differently. Not only was he incredibly respectful, but his films have also won a lot of awards. The leading actress was Jess Wexler, who gets burned as part of the plot, and I played her burn double as a supporting actress.

We filmed for about fourteen days in an old mental institution in Harrisburg, Pennsylvania, and also in Queens Park on Long Island in May, where, during a 12-hour shoot from six at night to dawn, all of the filming was outside, and it was absolutely freezing.

[*Aside from Jerry: This is the first time since the hospital that Diana had gone anywhere without me for any length of time. I missed her, sure, and I was worried. Actors and crews are notoriously known for their, shall we say, partying abilities. My worries were unfounded, as usual—while the rest were partying, Diana and another "friend of Bill" went to a meeting.*]

Still, I had thought it would be fun, and I was right. The best part was when we were in a holding—when we weren't on camera. I led yoga classes. There was a true bearded lady who taught us how to juggle. The film's star, Adam Pearson, did card tricks. It was a very entertaining group of people and one of the best experiences of my life.

Getting to attend the premier of the film at the Brooklyn Arts Museum, the "wrap" party in Brooklyn, and the theater premier in New York made the experience feel incredibly glamorous. The film received great reviews when it went on the international film festival tour, and I still see some of the other actors from the movie on TV from time to time.

The New Normal with Extra Gratitude

My expectations were reduced to zero when I was 21.
Everything since then has been a bonus.
—Stephen Hawking

<u>Diana</u>

Ninety percent of my body was burned in the fire.

I almost died.

These are facts.

They will be with me for the rest of my life, but they do not define me.

I am not the sum of my burns.

Before the fire, I had a life. I worked. I made mistakes.

I owned my own business. I became an alcoholic and recovered, and I did some charity work every now and again. The day before 9/11, I met the love of my life.

Chapter Twelve — *The New Normal with Extra Gratitude*

Since the burn, I've strived to help other burn survivors and advocated for those who had no voice.

I even became a movie star.

These, too, are facts.

The fire was the most horrible event ever to happen to me, and I'm forced to think about it every day as I work through the never-ending recovery process. But I've accepted that the fire was preordained. It was always part of my path to follow.

I celebrated my five-year anniversary of being sober at Spaulding Rehabilitation Hospital. I finished sponsoring an AA member in April 2023, learning that helping other alcoholics is like helping burn survivors; in its own way, it helps you recover from your own trauma.

And now, I have the knowledge of surviving the fire, which I can pass on to help others. Being involved with support groups, Burn Survivors of New England, and the Boston Harvard-Burn Model Systems have given me a sense of completeness, of coming full circle.

In September 2023, Jerry and I finally got married, starting a new chapter in our journey.

We wrote this book to help other survivors and their caregivers. Our experience comes from my burn story, but any survivors could use the information here.

My personal message is that there is a future—it just might not be the one you envisioned.

You can lead a life of purpose; you just might have to take a different path.

And you can find happiness again.

Before the fire, I thought I knew what success looked like—I thought I needed a college degree and a good job. But the kind of success I've enjoyed has no dollar signs or letters after my name.

While it's true that I'm not living the life I dreamed of in my youth, if you think about it, who really does that anyway?

I'm living the life I was meant to live. I'm with Jerry, and we're making the most of every second. It's a simple life—the kind of life that God intended for me.

Jerry

Today I continue to work at my brokerage company, merchandising cleaning products to distributors across New England. It has gotten more difficult with the cost of the goods and the raw materials to make them, as well as persistent supply chain issues, but I maintain in constant contact with my accounts, as that's the heart and trust of my business, serving clients.

Though I will draw my SSI in a bit, I plan to continue with work, as it satisfies me, gives me purpose—and keeps me busy.

Chapter Twelve — *The New Normal with Extra Gratitude*

I have gone back to school online to acquire a certificate in the counseling field. I am hoping to finish up by year's end and take the exam in early 2024.

I am presently working a few days a week in a Detox center and most days find the work rewarding.

Roman Emperor Marcus Aurelius once said, and I quote, "The impediment to action advances action. What stands in the way becomes the way." Adversity shouldn't be seen as a hardship, but as a challenge.

Diana and I can reflect on the adversity that has manifested itself in our lives and how we dealt with it. It could have destroyed us, made us resentful and discontent, but it did not. It shaped and motivated us to help enrich the lives of others with positive affirmations of our journey through fire.

Throughout our trials, I know my love for Diana, my wife, is the glue that has held me together, that has made me complete and whole.

God surely had not moved, and once we truly found Him, we knew that He most definitely placed us in each other's lives to save each other.

Final Thoughts

A Note from Diana

To Burn Survivors and their Caregivers:

Burns have been called the worst trauma that a human body can suffer. Any burn survivor of any burn size would instantly second that. Or, as burn degrees go, third it. And fourth it. (A little of my wit).

Surviving through such horrible trauma, the question is, what are you going to do with your "new normal"?

Are you going to drown it with alcohol or pain medications?

Are you going to stay in bed, wallowing in depression?

Are you going to live a 24/7 pity party?

Are you going to isolate yourself because you look different than "normal" people?

Normal—look around—what is normal?

Initially, we have to leave treatment and surgical procedure decisions up to our burn teams, but our emotional recovery is up to us.

The same goes for the people who love and support us, because they also are "burn survivors".

I was fortunate that I had a life partner/burn survivor, loving family, and many friends who stood beside me along the way. I was also fortunate enough to have caring, compassionate medical professionals who knew how important it was to introduce me to the burn community. It truly takes a village.

Other people who had been through the same hell I was experiencing shared with me a passion for life and for helping others. That's when the seed was planted that I could have a life, a good life, a life filled with helping others—a purpose that carried no monetary gain but filled my heart and soul.

It is true that no one understands a burn survivor except another burn survivor, just as no one understands an alcoholic except another alcoholic. So, find someone who understands you.

Learn your burn. Be curious, even though you may not understand the medical jargon or all the acronyms. Look them up. Ask questions! Learn your new body, and if it is telling you something is wrong, listen to it and follow up immediately.

Advocate for yourself. Burns and burn treatments are so complex that they affect every organ and every system in your body. What may be "normal" medical treatments for other people can be complicated for us. Find a way to take care of your health. If you don't know how to advocate for yourself, ask for help. Participate in research or volunteer!

Participate physically and emotionally in your recovery. Allow yourself to grieve. There is a big difference between your "old self" and your "new normal." We may get the best of therapy while we are hospitalized to regain what days, weeks, months, even years have taken from us. After discharge, it is up to us, no matter how painful and futile it may seem at times, to get physically active.

At first, it may be chair yoga or a walk that is excruciatingly painful, but I promise you that it will get better if you keep on trying. If it doesn't get better, guess what…Something's Wrong. Which means, rather than deny or ignore it, seek treatment.

Distraction is the best pain medication, at least for this burn survivor. Find a physical activity that you are passionate about. My theory is *not* to call it "exercise" 😁.

In a nutshell, self-care is tedious and time consuming, but well worth it in the long run. It *is* true that what doesn't kill you makes you stronger, and I'll add, "more compassionate, and more empathetic."

Calamities will build faith in your Higher Power and make it purer.

If you don't have one, I'll share mine with you. It is God through Jesus, and He's *big* enough for all of us. I have been called a "miracle" more than once, even by medical professionals. Proof positive.

Finally, from AA, the one and only rule in it:
Rule 62: Don't take yourself too damn seriously.

Life, even tragedy, is full of humor…laughing purges and puts things in perspective.

Don't just exist…LIVE!

Acknowledgments

Some say, "it takes a village".

For Jerry and me, it took a metropolitan city with all the infrastructure. We will attempt to be all-inclusive with these acknowledgments, but if we thanked everyone individually, the acknowledgements would be longer than the book. If you are one of the many people who helped us along the way, and you notice your name wasn't mentioned, please accept our apologies and know that you are important to us.

Thank you to our parents for living your faith and teaching us right from wrong. It may have lain dormant for a while, but the foundation was there. God never moved. We were just looking in the wrong places.

Thanks to our church family and churches literally all over the world for the continual prayers and masses when life situations were especially dire. Most especially, thanks to The Fall River Church of Christ and Shiloh Church of Christ, which held Mom, Debbie, and the rest of the family up.

Thank you to Mom, who is and always will be my rock.

To my sister Debbie, who showed me that no matter what your physical condition, you keep on living and never give up.

Thank you to the burn survivor community, especially George and Mylene, and burn survivors all over the world for showing us that there is life after burns. Thanks for sharing your emotional support and hope.

Thank you to AA fellowship for the prayers and shoulders to cry on and the tools for coping and living one day at a time. And for your friendship.

Thank-you, Yvonne, across the distance in Clarksville, Tennessee, for being with Mom when I couldn't be and for your continuing love and friendship for the past 35+ years.

Thanks to Mark B for bringing Jerry home and helping to clear the wreckage.

Thanks to Jeannine and Sharon for taking care of the fur babies.

Thank you to the burn team—Jeremy Goverman, Sean Fagan,

Colleen Ryan, Rob Sheridan—who really thought I had no chance to survive, but tended to me like I was going to live forever, anyway.

As well, to the MGH nurses and therapists who are still in our lives today: Katie, Crystal, Frank, Lisa, Rich, Vanessa, Leslie, and all the support staff. Thank you, nurse Edna, for taking on such a hard task.

Thank you to Jeff Schneider, friend, mentor, advocate for burn survivors, and rehab doctor. Along with my nurses, therapists, and nurses' aides—Amanda, Rachael, Sammi, Jame, Jess, Cara, Hermine, Eugenia, Chrispina, and oh so many more.

Thanks to the friends who made it a point to visit regularly throughout the thirteen months of hospitalization, even though they had busy lives of their own: Lynn, Penny, Paula, Lucy, Sue and Bobby, Dave, Phillis, Linda, and Jean. Not sure which group the staff called "the crazy ladies. Thanks to the "committee" that planned the fundraiser.

Thank you to my Viking classmates of Clarksville's Northwest High (1974), who were a constant encouragement and sent well wishes. Also, to my friends, business associates, and social groups in Tennessee.

Thank you to our writers, Laura Graves and Randall Surles.

And thanks to Catherine Lunardo for her assistance in helping with the big decisions.

And immense gratitude to our unofficial "publisher", who desires anonymity.

Most of all, thank you to all those friends who are still in our lives, who continue to encourage and laugh and accept us—scars, faults, and all.

Jerry's Prayers, Poems, and Songs

(During the horrible 400+ days until Diana finally made it back home, Jerry sought help among his AA and church communities, sharing with them the prayers, songs, and poems he wrote then, as we share with you now.)

Jerry's version of "All I Need is You" by Sonny and Cher

Some men follow rainbows I am told
Some men search for silver some for gold
I have found my treasure in your soul, Diana
All I ever need is you

You're my first love you're my last
You're my future you're my past
And you loving me is all I ask, Diana
All I ever need is you

Without love I'd never find the way
Through the ups and downs of every single day
I won't sleep at night until you say, Diana
All I ever need is you

Right now I'm sad and all alone
Just like a ship without a home
The love you gave me keeps me hanging on, Diana
All I ever need is you

You get well and come back home to me
I'll be there in every way you'll see
I need to have you back by my side, Diana
Without you it's such a lonely ride

Our love for each other is stronger than this burn
We have so much more of life to learn
I need to have you back in my arms, Diana
All I ever need is you.

The Good and The Bad Wolf

The good and the bad wolf reside in my mind.
The good wolf is loving, gentle and kind.
The good and the bad both exist there.
The bad wolf lives on resentment and fear.
They both are in conflict to gain in the lead,
The one that will succeed is the one that you feed.
The knowledge you gain in this program to share,
will strengthen the good wolf in times of despair.
So focus on the good that you can do for today,
And that in its actions keeps the bad wolf at bay.
Feed on the wholesome good things in life, there are lots.
Discard the negative, bad, evil thoughts.
The Creator is the solution if you seek you will see,
The answers you need to the problems that be.
His methods and actions though not always understood,
The wolf he responds to is the one that is good.

My Creator

My Creator, my Spiritual Father, all powerful, I praise Your name.
Your will is mine.
Guide me in the direction You choose for me, that I may be an extension of Your hand and conduct myself accordingly.
Grant me Your daily blessing to serve Your will, not mine.
Please forgive me for my failures and shortcomings.
Give me the insight and compassion to forgive others.
Free me from my resentments and open my heart to Your love.
Strengthen my defenses against the evils that present themselves that You may take me home in Your moment of choosing.
In Jesus' name I pray, Amen

Harmony

Now love is a word that is too seldom heard,
when we speak of our colleagues and such.
In our quest to gain power and ascend up the tower,
we forget all the lives we will touch.
Some will assist in the goals we pursue, and some will just get in

the way.
But if we stay humble and grateful and steadily climb,
it would ease all our tasks, wouldn't you say?
So be kind to your brother and love one another, a Godly man once he did say.
For success will prevail and you're bound not to fail
if compassion's a part of your day.

Reflect

There is nothing so sad as the man who fell short
In his journey through life in the goals that he sought.
All the sweat from his brow and the efforts he made.
All the structures he built and the groundwork he laid.
Rewarded by none for the things he had done,
Respected by few he had taught how to run.
When all said and done, had he really fell short,
To reflect deep inside he knew he had not.
For the course he had chartered, that others would sail,
He knew that in his heart they were bound not to fail.

The Gift

As I look upon life and the passing of time,
I'm inclined to believe it's a gift.
We're all given one package to do as we please,
But the contents you'll find has no list.
For the directions you take, and the choices you make,
May lead you to fortune and fame.
But if you sit back and wait and leave it to fate,
You'll surely be sorry it came.
Unwrapped and exposed it's a beautiful gift,
That constantly needs to be tended
Like a garment that's worn each day of our lives,
It sometimes needs to be mended
The secret you'll find is not when it came,
Or how much time has elapsed through the years.
But rather the fit that's tailored each day,
And the honor that's felt as it wears.

The Enlightenment
The problems I encountered in life were grand.
There were loopholes and detours in all I had planned.
I had no solutions to these things that arose.
They left me dejected, stressed out, not composed.
I created a life of sadness and pain,
and sedated myself with alcohol in which to refrain.
I realize now that I lived in the past,
Fearful the future was arriving too fast.
If we live in the present, we control our own fate.
Of this I am certain, I have no debate.
By changing ourselves, our environment will change too.
It's a reflection of us our whole lives through.
Today, to be part of the universe in touch with all it entails,
I'm at peace with myself and content I'll prevail.
Each day brings new challenges to embrace and explore,
To seek out new goals in which to deplore.
Meditating each day, I find myself in deep thought,
With all the good fortunes existence has brought.

Photographs

In 2007, Jerry and Diana vacationing in Cabo San Lucas.

With Tennessee BFF Yvonne in 2004.

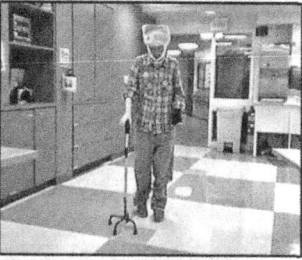

Using a 3-pronged walker at Spaulding.

5th floor Spaulding staff upon learneng that U.S. News ranked the hospital #1 nationwide.

Accompanying Jerry on a business trip in 2014, Diana came across this Smoky Bear and just could not resist the irony.

Five years after the accident, at a Summer Evening Concert at the Pier, where Diana and Jerry would run into a firefighter who had been one of the first on the scene that horrible day. The man teared up, moved that Diana was not only alive but out and about thriving, when that day those few tears earlier he'd assumed that she was a goner.

In 2014, Jerry & Diana in character heading off to the George Strait, Faith Hill, Tim McGraw concert at Gillette Stadium.

About a year after coming home, Diana was witness to her rock Jerry at his baptism at their Fall River Church of Christ.

Visiting Mom in Tennessee two years after the accident..

The New Normal, of course, must include joining Jerrry to watch his beloved Patriots.

Dr. Jeremy Goverman, wife Einav and their son Aitan in 2013. Dr. Goverman had by then become Diana's primary surgeon, and remains so today.

During the Covid lockdown in 2020, Presentation of Tablet for Patient Use and for Peer Support. (L–R): Dennis Costin of the Boston Firefighters Burn Foundation; Dr. Jeffrey Schneider; Diana, President of Burn Survivors of New England; and Meredith Chaney, Physcians Assistant.

Amanda Darling, Diana's "hugging RN" at Spaulding.

Diana cuts the ribbon, opening the Mass General Sumner Redstone Burn Center. One to always find the humor in any situation, Diana hesitated taking the scissors, asking CEO Peter Slavin, "Are you sure? I'm a little accident prone."

Circa 2019, Diana is with Haley (center) and Jenn, the mother of Haley's boyfriend Brandon, who was burned along with Haley at a gasoline-induced pit fire.

[An animal lover and veterinary assistant who had just signed a modeling contract before the accident, Haley delved back into her vet work within a couple of months of leaving the hospital. And she and Brandon are still a couple.]

Filming *Chained for Life*. Star Jess Wexler (R) with her stunt double Diana.

Diana, flanked by her sister Debbie and Deb's husband Gary. And Mom. 2013 in Massachusetts.

In Newport, Rhode Island, 2015, Diana and Jerry in the summer sun for a boat tour with one of Jerry's business associates.

2012. At home two years after the burn.

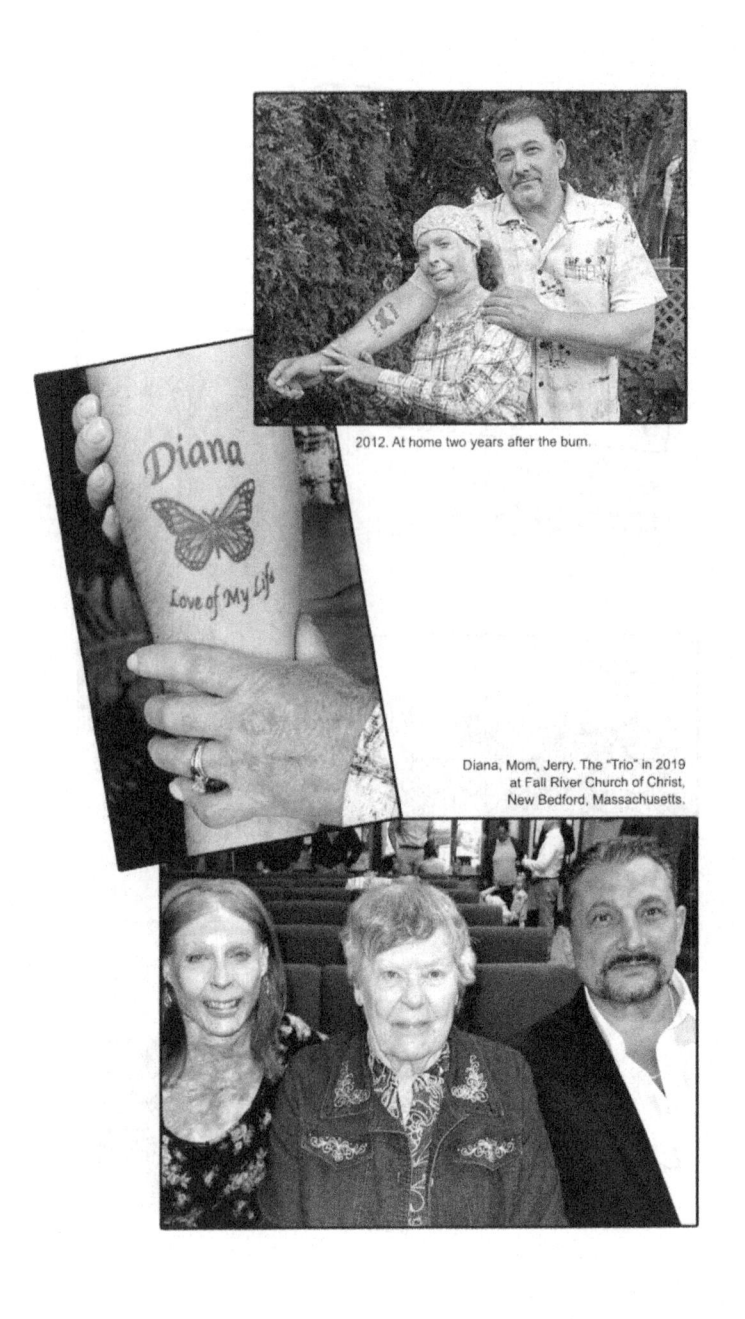

Diana, Mom, Jerry. The "Trio" in 2019 at Fall River Church of Christ, New Bedford, Massachusetts.

About the Authors

Diana Tenney is a 94% burn survivor, mostly 3rd degree, and spent most of the last 13 years working with other burn survivors and medical researchers. She is Past President, Secretary and Treasurer of Burn Survivors of New England; Co-Coordinator of Knowledge Translation for the Boston-Harvard Burn Model Systems; Event Coordinator for the BSONE Walk for Advocacy and Awareness; peer support certified; has participated and led presentations for the American Burn Society; leader for Wellness Rooms at Phoenix World Burn; participated in many burn-related videos as well as in an indie movie; and is active in Burn Research. She has been sober for 17 ½ years and is active in AA service.

Born in Manchester, TN in 1956, she left the South and for the past 28 years has lived in the Northeast.

Most of Diana's career was in outside sales, but she also worked at an auto transport company and a building supply company. In addition to her volunteer work, she is the bookkeeper for The Laperriere Group.

In her spare time, Diana is a Zumba and Yoga enthusiast, and she loves kayaking and gardening. She and Jerry tied the knot in a September ceremony at Kilburn Mills Event Center, on the rooftop deck overlooking the ocean, with both ministers from Fall River Church of Christ officiating. They plan to relocate to Tennessee to be with Diana's mom and her sister and family. Along, of course, with their dog Barney and cat Pebbles.

Jerry Laperriere is a 10% burn survivor and the husband of a burn survivor, Diana above.

He was born in New Bedford, Massachusetts in 1957. For the last 14 years, he has owned and operated The Laperriere Group Manufacturers Representatives and has earned awards for his sales abilities from the manufacturers he represents. He is studying to soon earn a certificate for addiction counseling, while presently sponsoring other men in Alcoholics Anonymous. He serves on the board of Burn Survivors of New England; the Boston-Harvard Advisory Committee and is certified to do peer support for burn survivors. He writes poetry, loves kayaking with Diana, and is a handyman around the house.

[**Laura Graves** and **Randall Surles** are professional book editors who consult, guide, encourage, and shepherd novice writers in getting their stories told, whether fiction (romance, sci-fi, mystery, action, military, historical), or non-fiction (self-help, memoir, science/tech).]

Made in United States
North Haven, CT
19 November 2024